PRIMA® GAMES

WE ARE STRATEGY

W9-AAC-732

FREE eGUIDE!

Enter this code at primagames.com/code to unlock your FREE eGuide:

2V9U-5HJX-CUVT-CH4X

CHECK OUT OUR eGUIDE STORE AT PRIMAGAMES.COM

All your strategy saved in your own personal digital library!

Mobile Friendly:
Access your eGuide on any web-enabled device.

Searchable & Sortable:
Quickly find the strategies you need.

Added Value:
Strategy where, when, and how you want it.

BECOME A FAN OF PRIMA GAMES!

Subscribe to our Twitch channel twitch.tv/primagames and join our weekly stream every Tuesday from 1-4pm EST!

*Tune in to **PRIMA 365** on our YouTube channel youtube.com/primagamesvideo for a new video each day!*

www.primagames.com

CALL OF DUTY
WWII

Call of Duty has been fighting its last few wars in the modern era and beyond, but here in 1945, it's back to basics. Personal drones and transforming weaponry have been replaced with entrenching tools and handheld radios.

In *Call of Duty: WWII*, each soldier on the battlefield has access to an assortment of specialized abilities, represented by the Division and Basic Training systems. With a broad arsenal of customizable weapons, each with its own array of attachable modifications, no two troops in the field will be alike.

MOVEMENT

There's a big difference between the single-player campaign and multiplayer *Call of Duty: WWII* and, as always, most of it comes down to movement. Against AI-controlled bots, you can afford to use standard infantry tactics, which means you can spend time standing still or using hard cover.

Human players, on the other hand, are much less predictable. If you spend any time standing still against a human opponent, you'll likely end up dead. The difference between the two game variations largely comes down to movement, so it's worth discussing the basics.

CROUCHING

This presents an enemy with a smaller target zone and stabilizes your aim. During close-quarters combat, this doesn't matter as much so you're likely better off staying on your feet. At long range, however, crouching can make the difference between life and death. Also, the Inconspicuous Basic Training lets you move faster while crouched. Also, the Inconspicuous Basic Training lets you move faster while crouched.

Crouching also makes your character's steps a little quieter. Sometimes, all that keeps you alive depends on who sees who first, so keeping a low profile can be a big help. Watch your corners and don't make any unnecessary noise.

GOING PRONE

Hold the crouch button to make your character lie on his or her stomach. If you do this while you're sprinting, your character throws him/herself at the ground in a dive, which can be useful if you're suddenly under attack from an unexpected direction.

Note, however, that being in the prone position dramatically limits your mobility. On the plus side, though, it makes you very difficult to hit from a distance and, as with crouching, stabilizes your aim. If you're exchanging fire with a target from across the map, it's worth the extra half-second to go prone, especially if you're using a rifle. At medium range, though, being prone just makes you a bigger target.

SPRINTING

As always, standard *Call of Duty* sprinting rules apply. You move faster and louder while sprinting and can only keep up the sprint for a short period of time. Members of the Airborne Division can sprint for longer distances without having to rest.

Generally, you can't do much else while sprinting, but some types of Basic Training will allow you to break that rule. Take **Gunslinger** if you'd like to fire while sprinting, or **Hustle** to reload while sprinting. You can also select **Energetic** for a shorter cooldown between periods of sprinting, as well as immunity to falling damage.

VAULTING AND CLIMBING

Hold the Jump button when approaching an object that can be climbed or vaulted to make your character automatically jump. You also receive an on-screen prompt whenever you're located next to an object that can be mantled. Before long, vaulting and climbing will become second nature.

MAKING A CLASS

As the start of your WWII career, you choose one of five Divisions. You begin with one class slot to customize and earn four extra slots early in your career (at Ranks 2, 4, 6 & 8). The standard Default loadouts from past Call of Duty's are now tailored around each Division's strengths. Each class features your choice of primary weapon, secondary weapon, Tactical or Lethal grenade, division, and basic training. Primary weapons have two Attachment slots by default, allowing even further customization. If you like, you can deck all your weapons out in the paint job of your choice!

WEAPON SELECTION

You can opt to bring a single shotgun, rifle (which, as a category, encompasses Semi-Automatic weapons like the M1 Garand as well as Automatic like a machine gun), sniper rifle, or submachine gun into the fray as your primary weapon.

With secondary weapons, your choices are simpler. You have the choice of a pistol (the 1911, P-08) or a machine pistol — or your trusty shovel. It's also possible to specialize in shovel-based mayhem by selecting the **Serrated Basic**.

After killing an enemy in the field, you can only swap weapons with the weapon the enemy was carrying when he died. Doing so does not replace a weapon in your loadout and, if you die, you respawn with your original weapon selection.

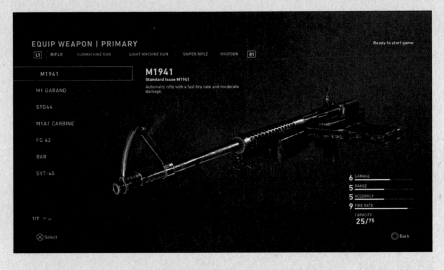

ATTACHMENT SELECTION

Every primary weapon (except the shovel) has a full list of potential attachments that you can — and should — install before heading into battle. You can install them from the same window used to select your weapons, in the small joined panes next to the weapon's window.

It doesn't cost anything to install an attachment once it's unlocked, so there's no reason not to use every one available. Note that when an attachment or weapon causes "extra damage against streaks" (such as Full Metal Jacket rounds), that means you inflict damage against scorestreak-related equipment and objects such as recon planes.

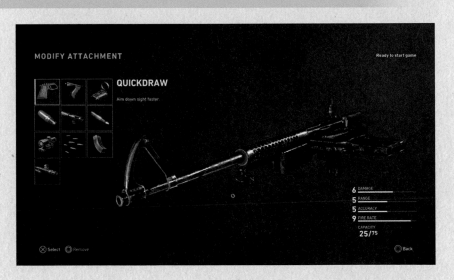

DIVISION SELECTION

Your soldier can opt to join one of five divisions, each of which confers four passive bonuses, in addition to access to one special weapon and basic training that you receive when you Prestige your division.

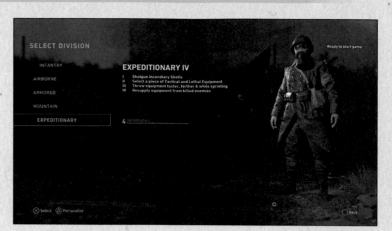

As a general rule, each division's passive skills "nudge" them in the direction of a particular gameplay style and weapon choice. Infantry gives players access to better weaponry and additional ammo; Airborne is ideal for players who like run-and-gun and "cavalry tactics;" the Armored division wields a giant machine gun and takes more explosive damage; Mountain soldiers are natural snipers and stealth operatives; and the Expeditionary squad are lethal when fighting at close quarters.

It's not all doom and gloom if you like to mix and match gameplay styles with abilities. For example, Mountain's passive ability that lets you sprint in silence can be useful on smaller maps that aren't great for snipers, but you definitely want to work with your Division's strengths.

BASIC TRAINING SELECTION

To further your combat potential, you can choose one of 21 types of Basic Training (five of which are unlocked via division Prestige), each of which conveys a passive benefit and/or a new type of equipment.

In the event that your Basic Training replicates a passive skill from your choice of Division, it's indicated in the menu instead of the Basic Training's effect. You can take it anyway, of course, but there's no reason to do so; doubling up on similar buffs doesn't "stack." The Division's version of the skill is always slightly better than the Basic Training's.

EQUIPMENT SELECTION

Lastly, you can pick a type of thrown equipment. By default, you spawn with one throwing item, although there are a number of abilities you can pick to expand your maximum or the number of items you can carry.

Try to customize your equipment for the map and the mode you're playing. Team Deathmatch isn't the best place for non-lethal "grenades," for example, and if you're playing against a bunch of bots, they tend to ignore smoke.

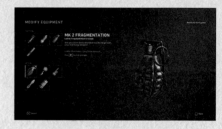

On the other hand, when you know a bunch of enemies are going to congregate in a single location, such as in Hardpoint or Domination, you can bring frag grenades to flush them out, or satchel charges and mines to defend your flanks from the enemy.

UNLOCK TOKEN

You'll get an Unlock Token each time your rank goes up. These tokens are non-refundable, so you can only use them one time to unlock a weapon, Division, attachment or Lethal/Tactical Equipment. Make sure to consider your options before throwing an Unlock Token into an item.

SCORESTREAKS

Sometimes, you need an edge. Scorestreaks reward your performance by allowing you to call in support from outside the battlefield, whether it's equipment, cover fire, AI backup, or a bombing run.

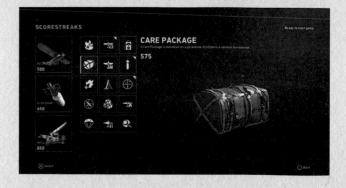

You can set any three Scorestreaks before entering a match, which automatically arrange themselves in ascending order of their cost. Your progress towards your Scorestreaks is reset to zero if you die. You can hedge that bet with certain types of Basic Training but, in general, the system rewards conservative and skillful play.

It's important to note here, especially for newcomers, that the points you earn towards a Scorestreak are not consumed when the Scorestreak is used. You aren't paying for the Scorestreak out of a pool of accumulated points; instead, you're just unlocking it. If you use a cheap Scorestreak early on, you aren't harming your progress towards the more expensive ones.

Most of the Scorestreaks are not intended to be equally useful in all situations. *Call of Duty's* maps and modes are designed to encourage players to be flexible and adjust their loadouts as required for their current game. You should tailor your approach accordingly, switching out your Scorestreaks as required for your skill level, character build, and current game type. If you know you're going to spend a lot of time in close-quarters combat, for example, that's when you want to pick a Flamethrower.

COMBAT

Up until now, we've been talking about preparation and planning. Now it's time to discuss performance: the action you'll see in the European theater and beyond!

AIMING

In *Call of Duty: WWII*, your weapons are period-accurate representations of the firearms and equipment available to soldiers in World War II. You get to fire classics like the M1 Garand and M1928 submachine gun.

That also means you must manage those weapons' drawbacks. Without appropriate specialization, many of the firearms in the game are surprisingly inaccurate when fired from the hip. In close-quarters combat, that isn't as important. At medium to long range, however, you should get into the habit of stabilizing your weapon. By crouching or going prone, as well as using your gun's iron sights, you can control your weapon and vastly improve its accuracy.

As a rule of thumb, fully automatic weapons (like SMGs) are most useful when fired in short bursts. *Call of Duty: WWII* accurately represents real-world physics such as muzzle climb, which means the longer you hold down the trigger, the higher the barrel of your weapon will go. It's surprisingly easy to burn off an entire clip in close quarters without actually hitting anything.

SPECIALIZATION

Although touched upon previously, it's important to note again: the game's systems are not designed to let you find a preferred approach and stick to it. The game encourages you to change up your arsenal, abilities, attachments, and equipment based upon the map, mode, and your team's goals. Not every map lends itself to every possible approach, so you are expected to match the game's flexibility with flexibility of your own. It's part of why you're given five create-a-soldier slots.

For example, the Gustav Cannon map presents a sniper with a wealth of opportunities as long as he or she can take and hold the high ground. The middle of the map is a huge, open area, which makes it difficult for short-ranged builds to get anything done. Try to charge a guy and he will pick you off from twenty yards.

Conversely, the Carentan map has precious few places where a sniper can hide and hold useful vantage points. It also features a wealth of blind corners and low fences, which makes a fast-moving, short-range specialist truly lethal.

You can split the difference here and go with an all-around contender build (Airborne or Infantry with Forage and a decent SMG or rifle, for example), but you tend to perform better in *Call of Duty: WWII* if you specialize for a particular situation.

FIRING RANGE

This chapter contains the information you need to create a class worthy of battle. You'll find listings and explanations for Basic Training, Primary and Secondary weapons including attachments, and Scorestreak descriptions.

PRIMARY WEAPONS

These are your bread and butter firearms that you'll spend most of your time tweaking and using during your time with *Call of Duty: World War II*.

RIFLES

Without a doubt, rifles are the most versatile weapons in the game. Although close quarters and wide-open areas may not be the most favorable conditions for a rifle user, they are still completely manageable. Whereas a shotgun would have little chance of winning against a sniper in an open area, or sniper against a shotgun user in tight quarters, the rifle can manage both while only being at a slight disadvantage.

To get the most out of your rifles, consider using **Scoped, Lookout** or **Forage** as your Basic Training. Rifles are flexible enough that you can try out some of the other more nuanced Basic Training options, such as **Ordnance** or **Espionage** instead of trying to actively improve your rifle usage.

M1941

Acquired: Unlocked from the start.

BASE STATS

NAME	STAT AMOUNT
Damage	6
Range	5
Accuracy	5
Fire Rate	9
Capacity	25/75

The low recoil of the M1941 allows for great accuracy at longer ranges. Adding the Advanced Rifling attachment greatly increases the full damage range of the gun, while Reflex Sight helps acquire targets at ranges greater than most other automatic rifles. Optionally, the 4x Optic can take the place of the Reflex Sight on maps with plenty of open land.

ATTACHMENTS

NAME	LEVEL REQUIREMENT	DESCRIPTION	STAT CHANGES
Quickdraw	Weapon Level 2	Aim down sight faster.	—
Grip	Weapon Level 3	Reduces weapon recoil while aiming down sight.	+3 Accuracy
Reflex Sight	Weapon Level 4	Basic Reflex sight with clear view.	+1 Range, +2 Accuracy
High Caliber	Weapon Level 5	Increases head shot damage.	+3 Damage
Steady Aim	Weapon Level 6	Better accuracy when firing from the hip.	+3 Accuracy
Full Metal Jacket	Weapon Level 7	Increases damage through surfaces. Extra damage against streaks.	+3 Damage
4x Optic	Weapon Level 8	4x Enhanced Zoom	+1 Range, +1 Accuracy
Rapid Fire	Weapon Level 9	Increases weapon fire rate.	+3 Fire Rate
Extended Mag	Weapon Level 10	Increases your weapon's magazine size.	—
Advanced Rifling	Weapon Level 11	Increases damage falloff range.	+3 Range

M1 Garand

Acquired: Unlocked by using an Unlock Token.

BASE STATS

NAME	STAT AMOUNT
Damage	8
Range	7
Accuracy	6
Fire Rate	4
Capacity	8/24

You know this rifle. You know it even if you can't remember its name or what it looks like. If looking at it doesn't immediately bring you back to every piece of World War II media you've ever seen, then the wonderful "*CHING*" sound of the clip ejecting from the gun will certainly remind you. The reason this gun is iconic is because it's stable, reliable, and punches holes through axis troops like they're made of paper. Hustle or Forage will make for excellent Basic Training, while Quickdraw and Extended Magazine make this a solid weapon for short to mid-range combat. If you're looking to do a bit of sharpshooting, then swap out Quickdraw for 4x Optic or Reflex Sight, depending on how far out you're expecting to be shooting.

ATTACHMENTS

NAME	LEVEL REQUIREMENT	DESCRIPTION	STAT CHANGES
Lens Sight	Weapon Level 2	Lens sight scope.	+1 Accuracy
Quickdraw	Weapon Level 3	Aim down sight faster.	—
Grip	Weapon Level 4	Reduces weapon recoil while aiming down sight.	+3 Accuracy
Reflex Sight	Weapon Level 5	Reflex Sight	Basic Reflex sight with clear view.
High Caliber	Weapon Level 6	Increases head shot damage.	+3 Damage
Steady Aim	Weapon Level 7	Better accuracy when firing from the hip.	+3 Accuracy
Full Metal Jacket	Weapon Level 8	Increases damage through surfaces. Extra damage against streaks.	+3 Damage
4x Optic	Weapon Level 9	4x Enhanced Zoom	4x Enhanced Zoom
Rapid Fire	Weapon Level 10	Increases weapon fire rate.	+3 Fire Rate
Extended Mag	Weapon Level 11	Increases your weapon's magazine size.	—
Advanced Rifling	Weapon Level 12	Increases damage falloff range.	+3 Range

STG44

Acquired: Unlocked at Technician Fourth Grade I (Rank 15).

BASE STATS

NAME	STAT AMOUNT
Damage	6
Range	5
Accuracy	6
Fire Rate	8
Capacity	30/90

With an exceedingly high rate of fire, the STG 44 is excellent for unleashing a lot of lead before your enemies have time to retaliate. With the Grip and Extended Mag, you'll immediately get the advantage in a firefight the moment you enter the fray. The Grip helps compensate for the fast fire rate, while the Extended Mag allows you to stay in combat, ready for the next threat that enters the area.

ATTACHMENTS

NAME	LEVEL REQUIREMENT	DESCRIPTION	STAT CHANGES
Lens Sight	Weapon Level 2	Lens sight scope.	+1 Accuracy
Quickdraw	Weapon Level 3	Aim down sight faster.	—
Grip	Weapon Level 4	Reduces weapon recoil while aiming down sight.	+3 Accuracy
Reflex Sight	Weapon Level 5	Basic Reflex sight with clear view.	+1 Range, +2 Accuracy
High Caliber	Weapon Level 6	Increases head shot damage.	+3 Damage
Steady Aim	Weapon Level 7	Better accuracy when firing from the hip.	+3 Accuracy
Full Metal Jacket	Weapon Level 8	Increases damage through surfaces. Extra damage against streaks.	+3 Damage
4x Optic	Weapon Level 9	4x Enhanced Zoom	+1 Range, +1 Accuracy
Rapid Fire	Weapon Level 10	Increases weapon fire rate.	+3 Fire Rate
Extended Mag	Weapon Level 11	Increases your weapon's magazine size.	—
Advanced Rifling	Weapon Level 12	Increases damage falloff range.	+3 Range

M1A1 Carbine

Acquired: Unlocked at Technical Sergeant I (Rank 31).

BASE STATS

NAME	STAT AMOUNT
Damage	6
Range	7
Accuracy	8
Fire Rate	4
Capacity	15/45

You must land three shots in a row to take down an enemy with full health, thus you need to shoot quickly and accurately to bring an opponent down. The gun is fairly accurate, meaning you can get by with just the iron sights. Adding Rapid Fire allows for quicker shots. Using Advanced Rifling allows you to maintain lethality at range without bringing you into the four-shot kill territory.

ATTACHMENTS

NAME	LEVEL REQUIREMENT	DESCRIPTION	STAT CHANGES
Lens Sight	Weapon Level 2	Lens sight scope.	+1 Accuracy
Quickdraw	Weapon Level 3	Aim down sight faster.	—
Grip	Weapon Level 4	Reduces weapon recoil while aiming down sight.	+3 Accuracy
Reflex Sight	Weapon Level 5	Basic Reflex sight with clear view.	+1 Range, +2 Accuracy
High Caliber	Weapon Level 6	Increases head shot damage.	+3 Damage
Steady Aim	Weapon Level 7	Better accuracy when firing from the hip.	+3 Accuracy
Full Metal Jacket	Weapon Level 8	Increases damage through surfaces. Extra damage against streaks.	+3 Damage
4x Optic	Weapon Level 9	4x Enhanced Zoom	+1 Range, +1 Accuracy
Rapid Fire	Weapon Level 10	Increases weapon fire rate.	+3 Fire Rate
Extended Mag	Weapon Level 11	Increases your weapon's magazine size.	—
Advanced Rifling	Weapon Level 12	Increases damage falloff range.	+3 Range

FG 42

Acquired: Unlocked at Captain (Rank 45).

BASE STATS

NAME	STAT AMOUNT
Damage	7
Range	7
Accuracy	6
Fire Rate	5
Capacity	20/60

Powerful, stable and reliable when fired from the hip, this is a very solid and versatile rifle that is much more effective at short and mid-range compared to most other rifles. Attach Steady Aim to emphasize the hip fire accuracy for close-quarters combat and a Reflex Sight for mid-ranged play if you want to utilize the unique traits of this weapon to their fullest.

ATTACHMENTS

NAME	LEVEL REQUIREMENT	DESCRIPTION	STAT CHANGES
Quickdraw	Weapon Level 2	Aim down sight faster.	—
Grip	Weapon Level 3	Reduces weapon recoil while aiming down sight.	+3 Accuracy
Reflex Sight	Weapon Level 4	Basic reflex sight with clear view.	+1 Range, +2 Accuracy
High Caliber	Weapon Level 5	Increases head shot damage.	+3 Damage
Steady Aim	Weapon Level 6	Better accuracy when firing from the hip.	+3 Accuracy
Full Metal Jacket	Weapon Level 7	Increases damage through surfaces. Extra damage against streaks.	+3 Damage
4x Optic	Weapon Level 8	4x Enhanced Zoom	+1 Range, +1 Accuracy
Rapid Fire	Weapon Level 9	Increases weapon fire rate.	+3 Fire Rate
Extended Mag	Weapon Level 10	Increases your weapon's magazine size.	—
Advanced Rifling	Weapon Level 11	Increases damage falloff range.	+3 Range

BAR

BASE STATS

NAME	STAT AMOUNT
Damage	7
Range	6
Accuracy	5
Fire Rate	7
Capacity	20/60

This is an excellent all-around weapon that can be built to fit your desired play style. Slap a Reflex Sight and a Grip or Advanced Rifling for better mid-ranged play, or add an Extended Mag and Rapid Fire for a more rush-oriented style of play. The choice is yours with this weapon, so experiment and see what works the best.

ATTACHMENTS

NAME	LEVEL REQUIREMENT	DESCRIPTION	STAT CHANGES
Lens Sight	Weapon Level 2	Lens sight scope.	+1 Accuracy
Quickdraw	Weapon Level 3	Aim down sight faster.	—
Grip	Weapon Level 4	Reduces weapon recoil while aiming down sight.	+3 Accuracy
Reflex Sight	Weapon Level 5	Basic reflex sight with clear view.	+1 Range, +2 Accuracy
High Caliber	Weapon Level 6	Increases head shot damage.	+3 Damage
Steady Aim	Weapon Level 7	Better accuracy when firing from the hip.	+3 Accuracy
Full Metal Jacket	Weapon Level 8	Increases damage through surfaces. Extra damage against streaks.	+3 Damage
4x Optic	Weapon Level 9	4x Enhanced Zoom	+1 Range, +1 Accuracy
Rapid Fire	Weapon Level 10	Increases weapon fire rate.	+3 Fire Rate
Extended Mag	Weapon Level 11	Increases your weapon's magazine size.	—
Advanced Rifling	Weapon Level 12	Increases damage falloff range.	+3 Range

SVT-40

BASE STATS

NAME	STAT AMOUNT
Damage	8
Range	8
Accuracy	6
Fire Rate	3
Capacity	10/40

A slower rifle compared to its contemporaries, however, the SVT-40 packs a massive punch with impressive range. Slap a Reflex Sight and a Grip to really emphasize this weapon's strong suits. You may also consider putting an Extended Mag in place of the Grip to increase the weapon's low ammo.

ATTACHMENTS

NAME	LEVEL REQUIREMENT	DESCRIPTION	STAT CHANGES
Lens Sight	Weapon Level 2	Lens sight scope.	+1 Accuracy
Quickdraw	Weapon Level 3	Aim down sight faster.	—
Grip	Weapon Level 4	Reduces weapon recoil while aiming down sight.	+3 Accuracy
Reflex Sight	Weapon Level 5	Basic reflex sight with clear view.	+1 Range, +2 Accuracy
High Caliber	Weapon Level 6	Increases head shot damage.	+3 Damage
Steady Aim	Weapon Level 7	Better accuracy when firing from the hip.	+3 Accuracy
Full Metal Jacket	Weapon Level 8	Increases damage through surfaces. Extra damage against streaks.	+3 Damage
4x Optic	Weapon Level 9	4x Enhanced Zoom	+1 Range, +1 Accuracy
Rapid Fire	Weapon Level 10	Increases weapon fire rate.	+3 Fire Rate
Extended Mag	Weapon Level 11	Increases your weapon's magazine size.	—
Advanced Rifling	Weapon Level 12	Increases damage falloff range.	+3 Range

SUBMACHINE GUNS

SMGs are all about fast movement and quick firing at the cost of accuracy and stopping power. Most weapons in this category are categorized as short to mid-range; they are extremely effective when used within those distances. Know when to pick a fight (and, better yet, when to pull back and reroute to a new path) to ensure success with this weapon type. There's no shame in backing off and searching for fights that will favor your weapon more than an opponent's.

Forage is one of the most useful Basic Training options for submachine guns because of the high rate of fire. **Undercover** works incredibly well when coupled with the Airborne Division's SMG Suppressor, but selecting **Energetic**, **Hustle**, or **Gunslinger** will also serve you well.

Grease Gun

Acquired: Unlocked from the start.

BASE STATS

NAME	STAT AMOUNT
Damage	6
Range	6
Accuracy	8
Fire Rate	5
Capacity	30/90

The Grease Gun is a tactician's weapon that can be challenging to master, but it is incredibly effective once you learn about it. Attaching Advanced Rifling and Extended Mags allows you to engage enemies at mid-range, a distance at which other SMGs lose their punch.

ATTACHMENTS

NAME	LEVEL REQUIREMENT	DESCRIPTION	STAT CHANGES
Lens Sight	Weapon Level 2	Lens sight scope.	+1 Accuracy
Quickdraw	Weapon Level 3	Aim down sight faster.	—
Reflex Sight	Weapon Level 4	Basic Reflex sight with clear view.	+1 Range, +2 Accuracy
Grip	Weapon Level 5	Reduces weapon recoil while aiming down sight.	+3 Accuracy
Steady Aim	Weapon Level 6	Better accuracy when firing from the hip.	+3 Accuracy
Full Metal Jacket	Weapon Level 7	Increases damage through surfaces. Extra damage against streaks.	+3 Damage
Advanced Rifling	Weapon Level 8	Increases damage falloff range.	+3 Range
Extended Mag	Weapon Level 9	Increases your weapon's magazine size.	—
Rapid Fire	Weapon Level 10	Increases weapon fire rate.	+3 Fire Rate

PPSh-41

Acquired: Unlocked by using an Unlock Token.

BASE STATS

NAME	STAT AMOUNT
Damage	6
Range	5
Accuracy	6
Fire Rate	8
Capacity	35/105

Due to its large magazine, the PPSH allows you to fire from the hip without worry of immediately running out of ammo. This makes it a great gun for close-quarters, run-and-gun action. Steady Aim helps to keep your hip-fired shots in a smaller area, while the Extended Mag allows you to continuously fire while you approach your target.

ATTACHMENTS

NAME	LEVEL REQUIREMENT	DESCRIPTION	STAT CHANGES
Lens Sight	Weapon Level 2	Lens sight scope.	+1 Accuracy
Quickdraw	Weapon Level 3	Aim down sight faster.	—
Reflex Sight	Weapon Level 4	Basic Reflex sight with clear view.	+1 Range, +2 Accuracy
Grip	Weapon Level 5	Reduces weapon recoil while aiming down sight.	+3 Accuracy
Steady Aim	Weapon Level 6	Better accuracy when firing from the hip.	+3 Accuracy
Full Metal Jacket	Weapon Level 7	Increases damage through surfaces. Extra damage against streaks.	+3 Damage
Advanced Rifling	Weapon Level 8	Increases damage falloff range.	+3 Range
Extended Mag	Weapon Level 9	Increases your weapon's magazine size.	—
Rapid Fire	Weapon Level 10	Increases weapon fire rate.	+3 Fire Rate

Type 100

Acquired: Unlocked at Technician Fifth Grade II (Rank 11).

TYPE 100
Standard Issue Type 100
Automatic SMG with modest damage and longest range capability in class

5 DAMA
7 RANG
7 ACCU
6 FIRE R
CAPAC

BASE STATS

NAME	STAT AMOUNT
Damage	5
Range	7
Accuracy	7
Fire Rate	6
Capacity	30/90

Featuring the highest range in its class, the Type 100 is great for moving quickly through maps that have large corridors with medium-range encounters. Adding the Lens Sight and Quickdraw allows you to take advantage of the increased range of this SMG by increasing your accuracy and speed when aiming down the sight.

ATTACHMENTS

NAME	LEVEL REQUIREMENT	DESCRIPTION	STAT CHANGES
Lens Sight	Weapon Level 2	Lens sight scope.	+1 Accuracy
Quickdraw	Weapon Level 3	Aim down sight faster.	—
Reflex Sight	Weapon Level 4	Basic Reflex sight with clear view.	+1 Range, +2 Accuracy
Grip	Weapon Level 5	Reduces weapon recoil while aiming down sight.	+3 Accuracy
Steady Aim	Weapon Level 6	Better accuracy when firing from the hip.	+3 Accuracy
Full Metal Jacket	Weapon Level 7	Increases damage through surfaces. Extra damage against streaks.	+3 Damage
Advanced Rifling	Weapon Level 8	Increases damage falloff range.	+3 Range
Extended Mag	Weapon Level 9	Increases your weapon's magazine size.	—
Rapid Fire	Weapon Level 10	Increases weapon fire rate.	+3 Fire Rate

Waffe 28

Acquired: Unlocked at Staff Sergeant (Rank 27).

WAFFE 28
Standard Issue Waffe 28
Automatic SMG with high recoil and highest fire rate in class

5 DAMA
4 RANG
6 ACCUR
10 FIRE R
CAPAC

BASE STATS

NAME	STAT AMOUNT
Damage	5
Range	4
Accuracy	6
Fire Rate	10
Capacity	32/96

Although its range is limited, this is still an excellent SMG. You can use attachments to compensate for its lack of range, but it's better to play to the weapon's strengths by attaching Steady Aim for better hip-fire accuracy, and Extended Mag to get the bullets flying despite its low fire rate. Just remember: Don't pull the trigger until you're within shotgun range, as the odds are stacked against you at greater distances. Once you're close, though, your opponents will be dust the moment you pull the trigger.

ATTACHMENTS

NAME	LEVEL REQUIREMENT	DESCRIPTION	STAT CHANGES
Lens Sight	Weapon Level 2	Lens sight scope.	+1 Accuracy
Quickdraw	Weapon Level 3	Aim down sight faster.	—
Reflex Sight	Weapon Level 4	Basic Reflex sight with clear view.	+1 Range, +2 Accuracy
Grip	Weapon Level 5	Reduces weapon recoil while aiming down sight.	+3 Accuracy
Steady Aim	Weapon Level 6	Better accuracy when firing from the hip.	+3 Accuracy
Full Metal Jacket	Weapon Level 7	Increases damage through surfaces. Extra damage against streaks.	+3 Damage
Advanced Rifling	Weapon Level 8	Increases damage falloff range.	+3 Range
Extended Mag	Weapon Level 9	Increases your weapon's magazine size.	—
Rapid Fire	Weapon Level 10	Increases weapon fire rate.	+3 Fire Rate

M1928

Acquired: Unlocked at Sergeant Major (Rank 48).

BASE STATS

NAME	STAT AMOUNT
Damage	5
Range	5
Accuracy	6
Fire Rate	9
Capacity	30/90

This weapon has a high rate of fire and inflicts decent damage, but the recoil is out of this world! Attach a Grip to help mitigate some of that recoil and an Extended Mag to increase the amount of time you can fire. Without the Grip, it's best to use this weapon during close-quarters combat. With the recoil in check, this is an excellent SMG fit for most combat conditions.

ATTACHMENTS

NAME	LEVEL REQUIREMENT	DESCRIPTION	STAT CHANGES
Lens Sight	Weapon Level 2	Lens sight scope.	+1 Accuracy
Quickdraw	Weapon Level 3	Aim down sight faster.	—
Reflex Sight	Weapon Level 4	Basic reflex sight with clear view.	+1 Range, +2 Accuracy
Grip	Weapon Level 5	Reduces weapon recoil while aiming down sight.	+3 Accuracy
Steady Aim	Weapon Level 6	Better accuracy when firing from the hip.	+3 Accuracy
Full Metal Jacket	Weapon Level 7	Increases damage through surfaces. Extra damage against streaks.	+3 Damage
Advanced Rifling	Weapon Level 8	Increases damage falloff range.	+3 Range
Extended Mag	Weapon Level 9	Increases your weapon's magazine size.	—
Rapid Fire	Weapon Level 10	Increases weapon fire rate.	+3 Fire Rate

MP-40

Acquired: Unlocked at Airborne Division Prestige 1.

BASE STATS

NAME	STAT AMOUNT
Damage	6
Range	6
Accuracy	5
Fire Rate	8
Capacity	32/96

The MP-40 has a high rate of fire, but low accuracy (a common trait of most SMGs). Despite this deficiency, it is reliable and can take down enemies with ease, provided it's in the right hands. Try attaching a Grip and/or Advanced Rifling to lessen the accuracy issues. Extended Mag is useful on pretty much any SMG (this one notwithstanding) and a Reflex Sight adds improvement as well.

ATTACHMENTS

NAME	LEVEL REQUIREMENT	DESCRIPTION	STAT CHANGES
Lens Sight	Weapon Level 2	Lens sight scope.	+1 Accuracy
Quickdraw	Weapon Level 3	Aim down sight faster.	—
Reflex Sight	Weapon Level 4	Basic reflex sight with clear view.	+1 Range, +2 Accuracy
Grip	Weapon Level 5	Reduces weapon recoil while aiming down sight.	+3 Accuracy
Steady Aim	Weapon Level 6	Better accuracy when firing from the hip.	+3 Accuracy
Full Metal Jacket	Weapon Level 7	Increases damage through surfaces. Extra damage against streaks.	+3 Damage
Advanced Rifling	Weapon Level 8	Increases damage falloff range.	+3 Range
Extended Mag	Weapon Level 9	Increases your weapon's magazine size.	—
Rapid Fire	Weapon Level 10	Increases weapon fire rate.	+3 Fire Rate

LIGHT MACHINE GUN

Using LMGs is remarkably similar to using sniper rifles. Moving around isn't as dangerous when using LMGs, but it definitely doesn't play to this weapon's strength. In fact, it's much better to find an open area or a long, narrow lane to pull out your bipod and wait for enemies to march in front of your crosshairs. These weapons are powerful and have incredible ammo capacities. Use **Hustle** to increase reload time and **Rifleman** to bring a second primary weapon, which can help during unfavorable conditions like close-quarters combat.

Lewis

Acquired: Unlocked from the start.

BASE STATS

NAME	STAT AMOUNT
Damage	6
Range	7
Accuracy	7
Fire Rate	5
Capacity	47/94

The Lewis LMG is a fairly well rounded weapon. Although all LMGs are prone to high recoil, you can use the bipod to counter it to a certain extent. Using the Extended Mag and 4x Optic helps pin down enemies at long range and keeps lanes of combat clear. This is especially important in War matches.

ATTACHMENTS

NAME	LEVEL REQUIREMENT	DESCRIPTION	STAT CHANGES
Quickdraw	Weapon Level 2	Aim down sight faster.	—
Grip	Weapon Level 3	Reduces weapon recoil while aiming down sight.	+3 Accuracy
Reflex Sight	Weapon Level 4	Basic Reflex sight with clear view.	+1 Range, +2 Accuracy
Steady Aim	Weapon Level 5	Better accuracy when firing from the hip.	+3 Accuracy
Full Metal Jacket	Weapon Level 6	Increases damage through surfaces. Extra damage against streaks.	+3 Damage
4x Optic	Weapon Level 7	4x Enhanced Zoom	+1 Range, +1 Accuracy
Extended Mag	Weapon Level 8	Increases your weapon's magazine size.	—
Rapid Fire	Weapon Level 9	Increases weapon fire rate.	+3 Fire Rate

MG 15

Acquired: Unlocked by using an Unlock Token.

BASE STATS

NAME	STAT AMOUNT
Damage	5
Range	7
Accuracy	6
Fire Rate	7
Capacity	50/100

This LMG's fast rate of fire means it can tear through enemies in the blink of an eye, but at the cost of instability. To help reduce recoil, consider attaching the Grip. Tacking on the Extended Mag will keep you firing until the area is secure.

ATTACHMENTS

NAME	LEVEL REQUIREMENT	DESCRIPTION	STAT CHANGES
Quickdraw	Weapon Level 2	Aim down sight faster.	—
Grip	Weapon Level 3	Reduces weapon recoil while aiming down sight.	+3 Accuracy
Reflex Sight	Weapon Level 4	Basic Reflex sight with clear view.	+1 Range, +2 Accuracy
Steady Aim	Weapon Level 5	Better accuracy when firing from the hip.	+3 Accuracy
Full Metal Jacket	Weapon Level 6	Increases damage through surfaces. Extra damage against streaks.	+3 Damage
4x Optic	Weapon Level 7	4x Enhanced Zoom	+1 Range, +1 Accuracy
Extended Mag	Weapon Level 8	Increases your weapon's magazine size.	—
Rapid Fire	Weapon Level 9	Increases weapon fire rate.	+3 Fire Rate

Bren

Acquired: Unlocked at Corporal II (Rank 14).

BASE STATS

NAME	STAT AMOUNT
Damage	8
Range	8
Accuracy	6
Fire Rate	3
Capacity	30/60

A slower LMG than its peers, the Bren compensates for its lack of speed with an increase in damage and range. Use Rapid Fire to help its low fire rate and Grip to maximize the gun's impressive range.

ATTACHMENTS

NAME	LEVEL REQUIREMENT	DESCRIPTION	STAT CHANGES
Quickdraw	Weapon Level 2	Aim down sight faster.	—
Grip	Weapon Level 3	Reduces weapon recoil while aiming down sight.	+3 Accuracy
Reflex Sight	Weapon Level 4	Basic Reflex sight with clear view.	+1 Range, +2 Accuracy
Steady Aim	Weapon Level 5	Better accuracy when firing from the hip.	+3 Accuracy
Full Metal Jacket	Weapon Level 6	Increases damage through surfaces. Extra damage against streaks.	+3 Damage
4x Optic	Weapon Level 7	4x Enhanced Zoom	+1 Range, +1 Accuracy
Extended Mag	Weapon Level 8	Increases your weapon's magazine size.	—
Rapid Fire	Weapon Level 9	Increases weapon fire rate.	+3 Fire Rate

MG 42

Acquired: Unlocked at Armored Division Prestige 1.

BASE STATS

NAME	STAT AMOUNT
Damage	6
Range	5
Accuracy	5
Fire Rate	9
Capacity	50/150

The MG 42 is a powerful, stable weapon with excellent range. One downside is its reload speed, which is common amongst all LMGs. Attach Quickdraw and Extended Mag to get the gun up faster and make it fire longer.

ATTACHMENTS

NAME	LEVEL REQUIREMENT	DESCRIPTION	STAT CHANGES
Quickdraw	Weapon Level 2	Aim down sight faster.	—
Grip	Weapon Level 3	Reduces weapon recoil while aiming down sight.	+3 Accuracy
Reflex Sight	Weapon Level 4	Basic reflex sight with clear view.	+1 Range, +2 Accuracy
Steady Aim	Weapon Level 5	Better accuracy when firing from the hip.	+3 Accuracy
Full Metal Jacket	Weapon Level 6	Increases damage through surfaces. Extra damage against streaks.	+3 Damage
4x optic	Weapon Level 7	+1 Rang	+1 Accuracy
Extended Mag	Weapon Level 8	Increases your weapon's magazine size.	—
Rapid Fire	Weapon Level 9	Increases weapon fire rate.	+3 Fire Rate

SNIPER RIFLES

Patience and accuracy are two things snipers can't do without. If you have these traits, then consider yourself right at home with a sniper rifle. With this weapon, your job is to find a spot on the map with a long, open view of the surrounding area. Close-quarters are not your friend, so avoid them like the plague.

The **Undercover** and **Instincts** Basic Training options help keep you hidden and safe from enemy attacks. **Lookout** provides more intel on the mini-map and allows you to identify enemies from a greater distance. Use **Scoped** to reduce your gun's sway while aiming down the sights, or **Rifleman** to bring a second primary weapon to allow for safer transitions between sniping locations.

Karabin

Acquired: Unlocked from the start.

BASE STATS

NAME	STAT AMOUNT
Damage	6
Range	8
Accuracy	6
Fire Rate	5
Capacity	10/50

Not the strongest weapon in the sniper rifle category, however, the Karabin is a quality rifle nonetheless. It takes no less than two shots to kill an enemy, assuming you don't land a headshot. This is the only semi-automatic sniper rifle. Note that the 4x Optic scope actually decreases the range of this rifle, enabling it to work in mid-range combat.

ATTACHMENTS

NAME	LEVEL REQUIREMENT	DESCRIPTION	STAT CHANGES
4x Optic	Weapon Level 2	4x Enhanced Zoom	+1 Range, +1 Accuracy
Ballistic Calibration	Weapon Level 3	Reduces sway. (Sniper Rifle only)	+3 Accuracy
Full Metal Jacket	Weapon Level 4	Increases damage through surfaces. Extra damage against streaks.	+3 Damage
Extended Mag	Weapon Level 5	Increases your weapon's magazine size.	—
Rapid Fire	Weapon Level 6	Increases weapon fire rate.	+3 Fire Rate

Lee Enfield

Acquired: Unlocked by using an Unlock Token.

BASE STATS

NAME	STAT AMOUNT
Damage	8
Range	8
Accuracy	7
Fire Rate	2
Capacity	10/50

A powerful sniper rifle with a large magazine, landing a shot to the chest or the head with this weapon will result in a nearly guaranteed kill. Note that the 4x Optic scope decreases the range of this weapon, enabling it to perform well in mid-range combat.

ATTACHMENTS

NAME	LEVEL REQUIREMENT	DESCRIPTION	STAT CHANGES
4x Optic	Weapon Level 2	4x Enhanced Zoom	+1 Range, +1 Accuracy
Ballistic Calibration	Weapon Level 3	Reduces sway. (Sniper Rifle only)	+3 Accuracy
Full Metal Jacket	Weapon Level 4	Increases damage through surfaces. Extra damage against streaks.	+3 Damage
Extended Mag	Weapon Level 5	Increases your weapon's magazine size.	—
Rapid Fire	Weapon Level 6	Increases weapon fire rate.	+3 Fire Rate

M1903

Acquired: Unlocked at First Sergeant I (Rank 41).

BASE STATS

NAME	STAT AMOUNT
Damage	10
Range	10
Accuracy	4
Fire Rate	1
Capacity	5/25

The M1903 is a powerhouse that can kill with just a single shot. Although it has an extremely slow fire rate, the amount of damage it dishes out with each shot is absolutely worth it.

The attachments for this weapon depend on a player's personal preference. You can use Rapid Fire to help with the fire rate, but the increase in speed is minimal at best. We suggest playing this one straight, relying on attachments that are more specific to the overall sniping experience. Ballistic Calibration fits that criteria, but an Extended Mag isn't a bad option either.

ATTACHMENTS

NAME	LEVEL REQUIREMENT	DESCRIPTION	STAT CHANGES
4x Optic	Weapon Level 2	4x Enhanced Zoom	+1 Range, +1 Accuracy
Ballistic Calibration	Weapon Level 3	Reduces sway. (Sniper Rifle only)	+3 Accuracy
Full Metal Jacket	Weapon Level 4	Increases damage through surfaces. Extra damage against streaks.	+3 Damage
Extended Mag	Weapon Level 5	Increases your weapon's magazine size.	—
Rapid Fire	Weapon Level 6	Increases weapon fire rate.	+3 Fire Rate

Kar98k

Acquired: Unlocked at Mountain Division Prestige 1.

BASE STATS

NAME	STAT AMOUNT
Damage	9
Range	9
Accuracy	6
Fire Rate	1
Capacity	5/25

A powerful and accurate sniper rifle, the Kar98k can have its scope swapped for the Iron Sight attachment to allow for a standard rifle approach. The Full Metal Jacket and/or Extended Mag help you keep pumping round after round, even when the enemy jumps behind cover.

ATTACHMENTS

NAME	LEVEL REQUIREMENT	DESCRIPTION	STAT CHANGES
4x Optic	Weapon Level 2	4x Enhanced Zoom	+1 Range, +1 Accuracy
Ballistic Calibration	Weapon Level 3	Reduces sway. (Sniper Rifle only)	+3 Accuracy
Full Metal Jacket	Weapon Level 4	Increases damage through surfaces. Extra damage against streaks.	+3 Damage
Extended Mag	Weapon Level 5	Increases your weapon's magazine size.	—
Rapid Fire	Weapon Level 6	Increases weapon fire rate.	+3 Fire Rate
Iron Sight	Weapon Level 7	Standard issued rifle with no scope. Can't hold breath while using this scope.	—

SHOTGUNS

Shotguns are for those who like getting up close and personal during battle. These are high-risk, high-reward weapons that can take down an enemy with one or two shots… but can also result in death if you miss even once. To get the most out of these weapons, use Basic Trainings like **Hustle**, **Gunslinger** and **Energetic** in order to get around the map as quickly as possible and close the gap between you and your target. **Rifleman** allows you to bring a second primary weapon to win a fight, while **Forage** keeps this weapon's relatively small ammo pool consistently full. Finally, **Undercover** can be really effective at keeping enemies from seeing the trail of dead players you leave in your wake while also making you more difficult to identify when they are looking your way.

Combat Shotgun

Acquired: Unlocked from the start.

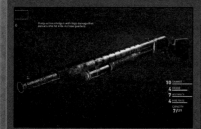

BASE STATS

NAME	STAT AMOUNT
Damage	10
Range	4
Accuracy	7
Fire Rate	4
Capacity	7/21

The Combat Shotgun is the most reliable and powerful shotgun at your disposal. While others offer more specialized firing capabilities, this weapon is a no muss, no fuss shotgun that becomes a hip-fire killing machine with the Steady Aim and Rapid Fire attachments.

ATTACHMENTS

NAME	LEVEL REQUIREMENT	DESCRIPTION	STAT CHANGES
Reflex Sight	Weapon Level 2	Basic Reflex sight with clear view.	+1 Range, +2 Accuracy
Quickdraw	Weapon Level 3	Aim down sight faster.	—
Steady Aim	Weapon Level 4	Better accuracy when firing from the hip.	+3 Accuracy
Extended Mag	Weapon Level 5	Increases your weapon's magazine size.	—
Advanced Rifling	Weapon Level 6	Increases damage falloff range.	+3 Range
Rapid Fire	Weapon Level 7	Increases weapon fire rate.	+3 Fire Rate

M30 Luftwaffe Drilling

Acquired: Unlocked by using an Unlock Token.

BASE STATS

NAME	STAT AMOUNT
Damage	7
Range	5
Accuracy	5
Fire Rate	8
Capacity	2/10

A double-barreled shotgun that packs a punch, the M30 can be as deadly to use as it is to be on the receiving end of its destructive shells. Unless you're right next to an enemy, it will take both shells to bring down a soldier. Miss a shot and say your prayers. To help alleviate this issue, equip the Rifle Bullet attachment to use in emergencies. Advanced Rifling is also a quality attachment to bring along for the ride. Hustle, Gunslinger, and Energetic are all decent Basic Trainings to use with this weapon.

ATTACHMENTS

NAME	LEVEL REQUIREMENT	DESCRIPTION	STAT CHANGES
Reflex Sight	Weapon Level 2	Basic Reflex sight with clear view.	+1 Range, +2 Accuracy
Quickdraw	Weapon Level 3	Aim down sight faster.	—
Steady Aim	Weapon Level 4	Better accuracy when firing from the hip.	+3 Accuracy
Advanced Rifling	Weapon Level 5	Increases damage falloff range.	+3 Range
Rapid Fire	Weapon Level 6	Increases weapon fire rate.	+3 Fire Rate
Rifle Bullet	Weapon Level 7	Enables rifle bullet to be used from the 3rd chamber.	—

Toggle Action

Acquired: Unlocked at Sergeant II (Rank 19).

BASE STATS

NAME	STAT AMOUNT
Damage	8
Range	4
Accuracy	7
Fire Rate	6
Capacity	6/18

A semi-automatic shotgun that deals far less damage than its contemporaries, the Toggle Action can be fired nearly as fast as you can pull the trigger. Rapid Fire and Extended Mag increase the firing capabilities tremendously, although you should consider Forage to help build up any lost ammunition.

ATTACHMENTS

NAME	LEVEL REQUIREMENT	DESCRIPTION	STAT CHANGES
Reflex Sight	Weapon Level 2	Basic Reflex sight with clear view.	+1 Range, +2 Accuracy
Quickdraw	Weapon Level 3	Aim down sight faster.	—
Steady Aim	Weapon Level 4	Better accuracy when firing from the hip.	+3 Accuracy
Extended Mag	Weapon Level 5	Increases your weapon's magazine size.	—
Advanced Rifling	Weapon Level 6	Increases damage falloff range.	+3 Range
Rapid Fire	Weapon Level 7	Increases weapon fire rate.	+3 Fire Rate

Model 21

Acquired: Unlocked at Expeditionary Division Prestige 1.

BASE STATS

NAME	STAT AMOUNT
Damage	6
Range	5
Accuracy	8
Fire Rate	6
Capacity	2/12

This weapon has great bullet spread, but low damage output when compared to other shotguns. There's no need to perfectly line up shots in order to deal damage, but it will take two shots in order to kill your targets — provided they were at full health at the start of your encounter. If one shot misses, you'll likely lose the fight. Advanced Rifling and Rapid Fire are good attachments, while Hustle, Gunslinger, or maybe even Energetic are all decent Basic Trainings to consider for this weapon.

ATTACHMENTS

NAME	LEVEL REQUIREMENT	DESCRIPTION	STAT CHANGES
Reflex Sight	Weapon Level 2	Basic reflex sight with clear view.	+1 Range, +2 Accuracy
Quickdraw	Weapon Level 2	Aim down sight faster.	—
Steady Aim	Weapon Level 4	Better accuracy when firing from the hip.	+3 Accuracy
Advanced Rifling	Weapon Level 5	Increases damage falloff range.	+3 Range
Rapid Fire	Weapon Level 6	Increases weapon fire rate.	+3 Fire Rate

ATTACHMENTS

Reflex Sight
Stat Change: +1 Range; +2 Accuracy

A simple sight that allows for better aiming and accuracy compared to the stock iron sights found on most weapons.

Full Metal Jacket
Stat Change: +3 Damage

Increases piercing damage through surfaces, making it easier to kill enemy troops hiding behind cover. As an added bonus, it also deals extra damage against vehicular Scorestreaks, like Recon Aircrafts.

Quickdraw
Stat Change: N/A.

Allows for a quicker transition between aiming down the sights and firing from the hip. Quickdraw is an excellent choice for rifles and SMGs.

High Caliber
Stat Change: +3 Damage

Increases headshot damage, a bonus that most players will find particularly useful. If you're not confident with your ability to get headshots, you're better off with a different attachment altogether.

4x Optic
Stat Change: +1 Range; +1 Accuracy

This is a scope with a 4x-enhanced zoom. This attachment is meant to allow for longer range potential on mid-range weapons.

Grip
Stat Change: +3 Accuracy

Reduces weapon recoil while aiming down the sight.

Steady Aim
Stat Change: +3 Accuracy

Steady Aim provides increased accuracy when firing from the hip (firing without aiming down the sights). It's especially useful when used in conjunction with shotguns and SMGs.

Rapid Fire
Stat Change: +3 Fire Rate

Rapid Fire increases the weapon fire rate for any weapon to which it's attached. Semi-automatic weapons don't benefit from this attachment as much as automatic weapons; this attachment is particularly beneficial for LMGs and SMGs.

Extended Mag
Stat Change: +50% Ammo Capacity

Increases your weapon's magazine size, which is particularly useful for shotguns and sniper rifles. It is also useful for weapons with a high rate of fire.

Ballistic Calibration
Stat Change: +3 Accuracy

Only for use with sniper rifles, Ballistic Calibration reduces muzzle sway while aiming.

Advanced Rifling
Stat Change: +3 Range

Increases the range a bullet can travel before its top damage is reduced. Advanced Rifling is excellent for getting more distance out of a decidedly mid or short-range weapon.

Rifle Bullet
Stat Change: N/A

Enables Rifle Bullet to be used from the third chamber of the M30 Luftwaffe Drilling shotgun. This is perfect for reloading emergencies, which are quite common with the Drilling's double-barrel setup.

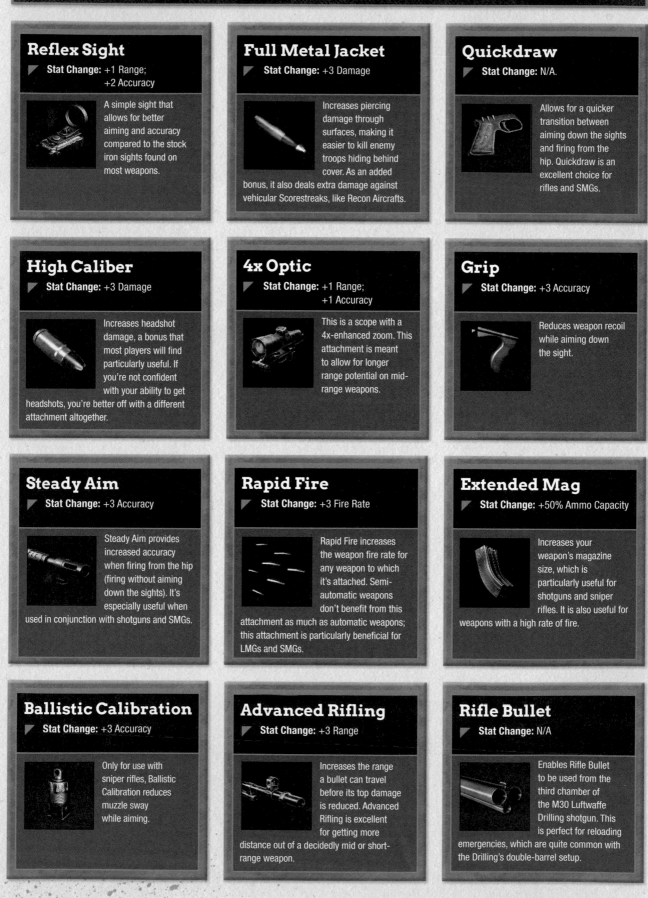

Iron Sight

▶ **Stat Change:** N/A

The Iron Sight is only an option for the Kar98k standard-issued rifle with no scope. You can't hold your breath while using this scope, so expect to use the Kar98k like a standard rifle instead of a traditional sniper rifle.

SECONDARY WEAPONS

When your primary weapon runs out of ammo, these are the weapons you're most likely to jump to. It should be noted, however, that there are also launchers and melee weapons that add a lot more diversity to your loadout other than just being a primary replacement.

PISTOL

The Pistol is a Basic firearm that is truly beneficial only when your primary weapon runs out of ammo.

P-08

◤ **Acquired:** Unlocked from the start.

STATS

NAME	STAT AMOUNT
Damage	6
Range	5
Accuracy	8
Fire Rate	6
Capacity	8/24

It's not the strongest sidearm in the bunch, but if you're looking for a pistol that is almost guaranteed to land its shots, this one will serve you well.

1911

◤ **Acquired:** Unlocks at Technical Sergeant (Rank 23).

STATS

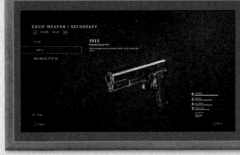

NAME	STAT AMOUNT
Damage	8
Range	6
Accuracy	6
Fire Rate	5
Capacity	7/21

Powerful, reliable and accurate, the 1911 pistol is a soldier's best friend when you're boxed in and running out of ammo. Aim well and you'll live to fight another day. Miss and you're just another dog tag.

Machine Pistol

◤ **Acquired:** Unlocked at Master Sergeant II (Level 33).

STATS

NAME	STAT AMOUNT
Damage	6
Range	4
Accuracy	6
Fire Rate	9
Capacity	10/30

The Machine Pistol has low carrying capacity, but an incredibly high rate of fire. Don't expect to go on a killing spree with it; however, it will save your skin in a pinch.

LAUNCHERS

Anti-vehicle and anti-personnel rocket-propelled explosive devices comprise this category. If you like weapons with a bit more spectacle, you've come to the right place!

M1 Bazooka

Acquired: Unlocked at the start.

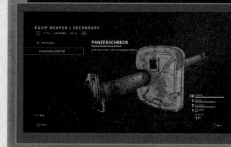

STATS

NAME	STAT AMOUNT
Damage	8
Range	8
Accuracy	8
Fire Rate	1
Capacity	1/1

The M1 Bazooka is probably used more for the purpose of bringing down enemy Scorestreak aircrafts than for taking out enemies on the ground. However, it works just as well to that end.

Panzerschreck

Acquired: Unlocked at Rank 18.

STATS

NAME	STAT AMOUNT
Damage	10
Range	7
Accuracy	7
Fire Rate	1
Capacity	1/1

Designed as an anti-personnel rocket launcher, the Panzerschreck is a powerhouse that can easily turn enemies into puddles of blood even with the most inaccurate of shots. Just don't liquefy yourself in the process!

MELEE

Melee weapons have all the power of a rifle bayonet, but without the need to be part of the Infantry Division.

US Shovel

Acquired: Unlocked at Command Sergeant Major (Rank 35).

You can take this one-hit kill melee weapon into battle as a replacement for a firearm, but the Shovel is better used when paired with the Serrated Basic Training. With it equipped, the Shovel becomes a primary weapon that you can quickly swing, meaning it's even more lethal than before. If you like the idea of using a primarily melee-based class, then this weapon is for you.

LETHAL EQUIPMENT

A wide selection of deadly, explosive, and throwable implements of war comprises this category. The Expeditionary Division is proficient with equipment, so keep that in mind.

Mk 2 Fragmentation

Acquired: Unlocked from the start.
Description: 6-meter blast radius; long throwing distance.

Your standard "pull, throw, duck" explosive device. You can hold the Mk2 after pulling the pin to "cook" it, thereby decreasing the amount of time it takes to detonate after throwing it. Just don't cook it too long, or risk blowing yourself up in the process. Use this weapon to clear rooms and groups of enemies, especially in the objective-based game modes like Hardpoint.

S-Mine 44

Acquired: Unlocked at Technician Third Grade II (Rank 22).
Description: 4-meter blast radius; maximum of two deployed at a time.

The S-Mine 44, or the Bouncing Betty, the perfect device for long-range players or those looking to raise some hell on the battlefield. While sniping, place one of these in a nearby path and you'll have peace of mind knowing that you'll hear enemies coming.

N° 74 ST

Acquired: Unlocked at Technician Fifth Grade I (Rank 9).
Description: 5-meter blast radius; 2-second fuse.

A sticky grenade that, once stuck to something (either an object or man), cannot be removed. If some poor soul is unfortunate enough to be on the receiving end of this sticky grenade, they'll have about two seconds to make their peace before getting blasted to pieces.

Throwing Knife

Acquired: Unlocked at 2nd Lieutenant I (Rank 37).
Description: 40-meter throw distance; can pick them up to use again.

Throwing Knives function like a ranged bayonet attack. Hit an enemy with a knife and they're DOA — no questions asked. It takes practice to master throwing knives, but with repeated use you'll gain the ability to silently take down enemies from up to 40 meters away!

Satchel Charge

Acquired: Unlocked at Lieutenant General (Rank 49).
Description: 6-meter blast radius; short throwing distance.

A remote-detonated explosive device, the Satchel Charge is perfect for holding choke points or protecting objectives. Place it in an area with high enemy traffic, or right next to a point, Bombsite or flag, then hit the trigger when you see an enemy within range.

TACTICAL EQUIPMENT

True to the name, Tactical Equipment is more about causing confusion in enemy ranks and limiting their visibility.

British N° 69

▶ **Acquired:** Unlocked from the start.
Description: 10-meter blast radius.

A stun grenade that dazes enemies for 2 to 4 seconds depending on how close they are to it when it detonates. It's an excellent gap closer for close-range situations and works just as well for close-quarters areas being held down by the enemy.

MK. V Gas Grenade

▶ **Acquired:** Unlocked at First Sergeant II (Rank 29).
Description: 4-meter radius; lasts for 5 seconds.

This grenade creates a cloud of gas that distorts and damages enemy players who get too close to it. It's particularly useful during close-quarters combat against enemies who are holding down a tactical location.

Smoke Grenade

▶ **Acquired:** Unlocked at Private First Class I (Level 5).
Description: 8-meter radius; lasts for 12 seconds.

The M18 creates a cloud of smoke that obscures the enemy line of sight. Throw it onto an objective, in front of a fortified position, or into an enemy defensive point to distract and confuse enemy players.

Signal Flare

▶ **Acquired:** Unlocked at Lieutenant Colonel (Rank 49).
Description: 6-meter radius; lasts for 5 seconds.

Creates a blinding light that gets more obstructive as you approach it. Get too close and you'll take damage, which adds an extra layer to the confusion it can cause when thrown into a crowded area.

BASIC TRAINING

Basic Trainings are extras a player selects to gain specific advantages in combat. You can only equip one per class, but most provide benefits that can offset weaker points of certain weapon classes, or help you acquire Scorestreaks more frequently. Picking the proper Basic Training is wholly dependent on your overall loadout, so craft your class before thinking about this step.

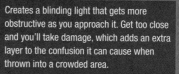

SELECT BASIC TRAINING

Ready to start game

▶ ESPIONAGE

LAUNCHED

REQUISITIONS

INSTINCTS

RIFLEMAN

HUSTLE

LOOKOUT

GUNSLINGER

ORDNANCE

PRIMED

3/21 ▼▲

REQUISITIONS

Scorestreaks do not reset on death, but cost more and can only be earned once.

INFANTRY IV
I   Rifle Bayonet
II Additional Primary Attachment
III Extra magazines
IV Move significantly faster while aiming down sights

⊗ Select

◯ Back

Launched

▷ **Acquired:** Unlocked from the start.

Take a Launcher (of the rocket-propelled variety) as a Secondary weapon and refill its ammo from defeated enemies. This works well if you're a big fan of explosions, or if you like shooting down enemy Recon Aircraft.

Forage

▷ **Acquired:** Unlocked at Rank 47.

When an enemy player is killed, he leaves behind small bags that can be used to refill a bit of ammo once. In addition, you'll swap and pick up weapons faster with this Basic Training equipped. It's not particularly effective for long-range loadouts, but it's especially effective when using SMGs and shotguns.

Lookout

▷ **Acquired:** Unlocked at Rank 20.

When using Lookout, enemies are identified at greater distances than normal and the range of the mini-map is slightly increased. It is particularly beneficial for those wanting as much information about the battlefield as possible and for those looking to play at long range.

Hustle

▷ **Acquired:** Unlocked at Rank 16.

With Hustle, the player reloads faster while sprinting .

Rifleman

▷ **Acquired:** Unlocked at Rank 12.

Enables you to take two primary weapons into battle and swap between them faster than normal.

Requisitions

▷ **Acquired:** Unlocked at the start.

With Requisitions, you don't lose your progress towards your equipped Scorestreaks upon death, but they cost significantly more to use and they can only be used a single time in a match.

Duelist

▷ **Acquired:** Unlocked at Technician Fifth Grade (Rank 43).

Take Akimbo pistols as a secondary weapon. Extra pistol ammunition.

Bang

▷ **Acquired:** Unlocked at Technician Third Grade (Rank 51).

Bang grants more capacity for your selected tactical equipment and allows you to take along an Mk 2 Fragmentation grenade.

Gunslinger

Acquired: Unlocked at Corporal (Rank 24).

Gunslinger allows you to fire your weapons while sprinting and diving, which is an advantage for SMG and shotgun builds.

Energetic

Acquired: Unlocked at Airborne Division Prestige 1.

Energetic consists of faster sprint recovery time and complete fall damage immunity. This one works quite well for close-up loadouts, but is useable for pretty much any build.

Espionage

Acquired: Unlocked at the start.

When you cause damage to enemies, they'll appear on the mini-map for a short period of time. If one of your teammates kills that enemy, you'll gain points for an Espionage assist. That's not all! This Basic Training also reveals enemy Scorestreak info on the minimap.

Ordnance

Acquired: Unlocked at Technical Sergeant II (Rank 28).

Your Scorestreaks cost less and you have the ability to re-roll any Care Packages you call in. It's not a must-have Basic Training by any means, but the ability to re-roll Care Packages provides an opportunity to get something sweet when you roll a small Scorestreak, like a Recon Aircraft.

Instincts

Acquired: Unlocked at Master Sergeant (Rank 3).

When using Instincts, a yellowish frame surrounds the outer edges of your screen when an enemy is targeting you from out of view. Although it doesn't point you in their direction, at least you know danger is nearby. It also reveals enemy explosive equipment, which is especially helpful against Satchel Charges and S-Mine 44s.

Undercover

Acquired: Unlocked at Captain I (Level 36).

While using this Basic Training, no opponent skulls are shown when you kill an enemy's teammate. Basically, they see nothing, effectively eliminating any trace of your dirty deeds. This is particularly useful when using an SMG with a Suppressor; your shots don't appear on the mini-map. So, no skulls means unless an enemy Recon Aircraft is in the sky, you remain invisible until someone actually lays eyes on you. Lastly, enemy reticles don't change when they are pointed at you.

Concussed

Acquired: Unlocked at Expeditionary Division Prestige 1.

You gain increased carrying capacity for your selected lethal equipment when using Concussed. In addition, you get to carry a Concussion Grenade as an added bonus.

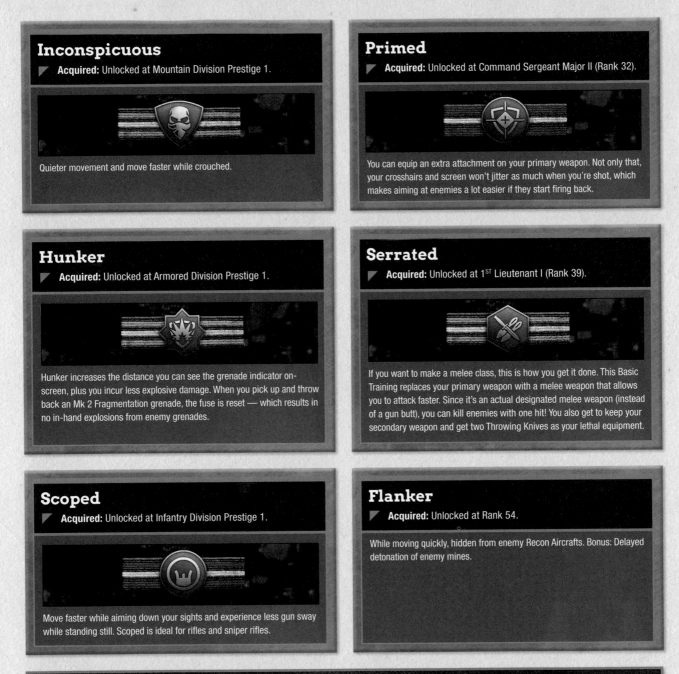

Inconspicuous

▶ **Acquired:** Unlocked at Mountain Division Prestige 1.

Quieter movement and move faster while crouched.

Primed

▶ **Acquired:** Unlocked at Command Sergeant Major II (Rank 32).

You can equip an extra attachment on your primary weapon. Not only that, your crosshairs and screen won't jitter as much when you're shot, which makes aiming at enemies a lot easier if they start firing back.

Hunker

▶ **Acquired:** Unlocked at Armored Division Prestige 1.

Hunker increases the distance you can see the grenade indicator on-screen, plus you incur less explosive damage. When you pick up and throw back an Mk 2 Fragmentation grenade, the fuse is reset — which results in no in-hand explosions from enemy grenades.

Serrated

▶ **Acquired:** Unlocked at 1ST Lieutenant I (Rank 39).

If you want to make a melee class, this is how you get it done. This Basic Training replaces your primary weapon with a melee weapon that allows you to attack faster. Since it's an actual designated melee weapon (instead of a gun butt), you can kill enemies with one hit! You also get to keep your secondary weapon and get two Throwing Knives as your lethal equipment.

Scoped

▶ **Acquired:** Unlocked at Infantry Division Prestige 1.

Move faster while aiming down your sights and experience less gun sway while standing still. Scoped is ideal for rifles and sniper rifles.

Flanker

▶ **Acquired:** Unlocked at Rank 54.

While moving quickly, hidden from enemy Recon Aircrafts. Bonus: Delayed detonation of enemy mines.

SCORESTREAKS

You accrue points by getting kills and assists and completing objectives. These points, which are added to your Scorestreaks, allow you to call in assistance from outside the battlefield based on the specific Scorestreaks you selected in the Class Creation screen once a certain point "cost" is reached. If you die before reaching the point cost for a specific Scorestreak, you lose all the points that were accrued toward that streak (they won't leave the scoreboard, just your progress toward your Scorestreaks). Therefore, playing carefully can be a real boon when you're nearing some of the more costly streaks. The Requisitions Basic Training prevents the loss of Scorestreak progress, but with increased Scorestreak costs and the inability to use a Scorestreak more than once a match.

When selecting a Scorestreak, it's important to consider the game mode you're playing. While Scorestreaks like Recon Aircraft are useful in most all circumstances, there are some Scorestreaks—including Recon Aircraft—that become even more useful depending on the game mode. While a heavy-hitter Scorestreak like Fire Bombing Run is killer in kill-based game modes like Team Deathmatch, it's even more brutal if you use it to cut off routes or prevent enemies from approaching points like in Capture the Flag or Domination. When choosing a Scorestreak, it's best to consider the game modes you plan on playing.

Molotov Cocktail

▶ **Acquired:** Unlocked at Private First Class II (Rank 7).
Cost: 300 points.

Molotov Cocktail is better used for cutting off enemy routes than for killing enemies outright, although they're still well suited for killing when an enemy takes a direct hit. If you want to force enemies out of a narrow path or opening, throw a Molotov at its most narrow point to force them to back off — at least for the few seconds that the Molotov Cocktail burns on the ground.

Care Package

Acquired: Unlocked at Corporal I (Rank 13).
Cost: 575 points.

When activated, you're given a red smoke grenade that calls in a supply drop from HQ. The supply drop gives you a random Scorestreak to use whenever you see fit; the catch, however, is that you must actually pick up the Care Package first. Enemy players are just as capable of picking up Care Packages, so throw the smoke grenade somewhere safe and isolated.

Recon Aircraft

Acquired: Unlocked from the start.
Cost: 500 points.

This Scorestreak temporarily reveals the locations of all enemies on the map. A radar scan flashes on the mini-map every 2 to 3 seconds, revealing enemy locations in the process. This Scorestreak works particularly well in objective-based game modes like Search and Destroy, Gridiron, and Capture the Flag.

Take note that your Recon Aircraft can be shot down by enemies if they use a launcher, a Counter Recon Aircraft, or a Flak Gun Scorestreak.

Fighter Pilot

Acquired: Unlocked at Staff Sergeant II (Rank 21).
Cost: 625 points.

With Fighter Pilot, call in a fighter plane and temporarily control it over the battlefield. Enemy team members will appear on-screen surrounded by red circles, indicating you can target them while controlling the plane. Steer the plane toward their location and hold the Fire button to unleash a volley of bullets. Be warned! This Scorestreak is ineffective on maps with a lot of interior spaces, such as Carentan.

Counter Recon Aircraft

Acquired: Unlocked at Command Sergeant Major I (Rank 30). **Cost:** 525 points.

A Counter Recon Aircraft is the simplest, most effective way to tear enemy Recon Aircrafts out of the sky. On top of that, they patrol for approximately the length of a Recon Aircraft, effectively screening any future Recon Aircrafts from taking flight. That said Counter Recon Aircrafts are better suited for game modes in which an enemy Recon Aircraft can put a damper on your plans, such as Search and Destroy. Outside of those, you're better off selecting something with a bit more oomph.

Glide Bomb

Acquired: Unlocked from the start.
Cost: 650 points.

This is the perfect Scorestreak for game modes (i.e., Domination, Search and Destroy, and Hardpoint) that force enemies into specific locations. If a point is being captured, or if you're having a hard time getting near a point, drop a Glide Bomb. Like the Fighter Pilot Scorestreak, it enables you to see the locations of most enemies on the map, so you can steer the bomb and drop it right on top of them.

Flamethrower

Acquired: Unlocked at Master Sergeant I (Rank 38).
Cost: 700 points.

The Flamethrower is a powerful, short-range Scorestreak. It's not the best one to take into open maps with limited cover (like Sainte Marie du Mont or U.S.S. Texas), but for maps that favor close-quarters play this Scorestreak is a monster. You can tear through enemies like their health is permanently set to 1 and you don't lose this Scorestreak until it is completely used up, even if you die!

Flak Guns

Acquired: Unlocked at 1st Lieutenant (Rank 42).
Cost: 950 points.

The ultimate support Scorestreak, Flak Guns block enemy aerial streaks after destroying the ones currently active. You won't get any kills with this one, but you can stop a Fire Bombing Run before it gets going if you time the use of this Scorestreak correctly.

Mortar Strike

Acquired: Unlocked at First Sergeant (Rank 26).
Cost: 750 points.

Mortar Strike is more tactical than Glide Bomb, with less influence on the projectiles themselves. You can select three separate locations anywhere on the map to drop mortars, although it should be noted that this Scorestreak almost demands that an ally Recon Aircraft be in the air before use.

Whereas the Glide Bomb provides a clean, top-down look on the battlefield, Mortar Strike reveals a rudimentary map from which to select your targets and enemies only appear if they fire unsuppressed weapons, or if a Recon Aircraft is in the air. Despite these shortcomings, this Scorestreak works well for objective-based game modes in which enemies are forced into grouping onto a specific location.

Emergency Airdrop

Acquired: Unlocked at Colonel (Rank 50).
Cost: 1000 points.

What's better than one Care Package? How about three? This Scorestreak drops three Care Packages wherever you throw the green-colored smoke grenade. You'll have three chances to get a particularly powerful Scorestreak, but at a much higher risk of theft. With three Care Packages on the ground, you not only have to worry about enemies shooting you and taking your hard earned Scorestreaks, but your own teammates can also collect them. It's best to find an isolated corner of the map before calling in the Emergency Airdrop, rather than risk losing your precious cargo to someone who doesn't play fair.

Artillery Barrage

Acquired: Unlocked from the start.
Cost: 850 points.

This is an excellent Scorestreak for splitting enemy ranks and controlling the battlefield. When used, Artillery Barrage sends waves of artillery rounds onto the selected spot on the map. Although it's not incredibly deadly, it is excellent for forcing enemies away from paths that might be disadvantageous to you and your team, or for pressuring them away from an objective. It lasts for a decent amount of time so, when used properly, it can mean the difference between success and failure in objective-based game modes.

Fire Bombing Run

Acquired: Unlocked at Major (Rank 46).
Cost: 1050 points.

Powerful, thunderous and persistent, the Fire Bombing Run is all the traits of a Molotov Cocktail magnified by 100 and squeezed into one long streak of fire. Use it to cut off enemy routes to an objective, or scatter them from a fortified position.

Paratroopers

Acquired: Unlocked at Technician Fourth Grade II (Rank 17). **Cost:** 1250 points.

No one said war was fair, which is why you shouldn't bother fighting fair yourself. If things are looking grim for your team, why not call for backup? The Paratroopers Scorestreak calls in a small troupe of AI-controlled soldiers to help turn the tides of battle. They'll run around the map and rack up kills for you. They may not be as deadly as a moderately skilled player, but there's always strength in numbers. Even the most battle-hardened veteran can find himself overwhelmed by the Paratroopers' superior numbers.

Ball Turret Gunner

Acquired: Unlocked at Major General (Rank 53).
Cost: 1700 points.

Ride in the gunner's seat of a plane high above the battlefield. Enemies appear on the map enclosed in a red circle, provided they are not inside a building or other structure. Simply point and fire to turn your foes into ash. This Scorestreak has an impressive length of time, making it a priority target for launchers and counter Scorestreaks held by the enemy team.

Carpet Bombing

Acquired: Unlocked at Sergeant Major II (Rank 34).
Cost: 1400 points.

A Carpet Bombing run hits the map with not one but three separate bombing runs. Once chosen, bombers will drop their bombs over enemy controlled territory or otherwise hotly contested areas. The delay between runs is significant enough that players can relocate after the first strike, but the wait time can make all but the most observant of players forget that this attack comes in threes.

DIVISIONS

At the start of your multiplayer experience, you have the option to select from one of five Divisions, or playstyles. Each one offers benefits and boons to all the weapons under a specific weapon category. Like rifles? Choose Infantry as your Division. Love fast running and SMGs? Select the Airborne Division. You aren't locked into only using the first Division you pick by any means, but you should carefully select your first Division. If you're not keen on a certain weapon type, remember that Divisions still offer small benefits to their associated weapon class. In order to unlock another Division to use as a replacement, you need to burn an **Unlock Token**. These tokens are better used on a new weapon or Basic Training.

After selecting a Division, there are a few things to note. Namely, your selected Division will level up along with your in-game character. As you level up your Division, you'll unlock new benefits for the weapon class your Division supports. Division benefits are available whenever you use the Division and don't require the divisional weapon class, too. As an example, selecting the Armored Division immediately gives all of your LMGs a bipod for stable prone and on-cover firing. Level it up to become immune to Shell Shock (the blur and ear-splitting squeal of an explosive blowing up nearby). Level it further to take less fire damage, and so on.

Experiment with the Divisions if you have extra Unlock Tokens. Only the first level of each Division is linked to their weapon class. All other "extras" unlocked by Divisions can be used with any type of weapon. Weapon and Basic Training are unlocked at Prestige 1 and can be used with any Division.

INFANTRY

The defacto rifleman's Division, Infantry starts off its members with a rifle bayonet for every rifle in the game. Use the bayonet for one-hit melee kills. Note that every other melee attack is two hits, unless you strike an enemy's back. Players can charge with the Infantry's Rifle Bayonet to close the gap on an enemy, but they will scream while charging, alerting enemies to your location. As you rank up this Division, you gain

LEVEL	DESCRIPTION
I	Rifle bayonet
II	Additional primary attachment
III	Extra magazines
IV	Move faster while aiming down sights
Prestige 1	SVT-40 Rifle & Scoped Basic Training

an additional Attachment slot for you primary weapon, extra ammo magazines, faster ADS (Aiming Down Sights) and, finally, the SVT-40 rifle. Infantry is the place to be for those who love attachments and maximizing their gun's potential.

AIRBORNE

Those who use SMGs regularly in *Call of Duty* know full well the joys of moving fast and catching enemy players unaware. Sledgehammer Games understands this, too. Select the Airborne Division to start all of your SMGs with a Suppressor that can be applied (or removed) at will. You'll lose a bit of top damage, but you won't appear on the mini-map when you

LEVEL	DESCRIPTION
I	SMG Suppressor
II	Sprint for longer distances.
III	Climb over obstacles faster.
IV	Increased sprint speed.
Prestige 1	MP-40 SMG & Energetic Basic Training

fire a weapon with the Suppressor attached. As you level up this Division, you gain the ability to sprint longer and faster and climb obstacles quicker. This is an excellent build for traditional CoD run-n-gun. The movement abilities are very handy for objective-based modes like War and Capture the Flag. Upon reaching Division Level V, you unlock perhaps the most recognizable German weapon — the MP-40.

ARMORED

Have you ever dreamed of being a one-man army? Of taking on the whole of the Axis with nothing but an LMG in one hand and its bullet belt in the other? Of basically being every great 80s action hero? Good news! There's a Division just for you and it's called Armored.

Staying true to its namesake, the Armored Division progressively makes you more resistant to fire and explosive damage, not to mention

LEVEL	DESCRIPTION
I	LMG Bipod.
II	Immune to Shell Shock and Tactical Equipment.
III	Take less fire damage.
IV	Take less explosive damage.
Prestige 1	MG42 & Hunker Basic Training

immunity to the shell shock effects of explosives and Tactical Equipment. You also receive an LMG Bipod for any LMG you select, which allows you to set up shop just about anywhere you can go prone or on any waist-high cover. This Division is great for objective-based modes. The protection from explosives is excellent.

MOUNTAIN

Silent, invisible and deadly at uncontestable ranges, the Mountain Division is where snipers are at their best. Working through this Division grants you the following: invisibility to UAVs; makes you untraceable to enemy Scorestreaks; and silent to the enemy's ears. Beyond that, you can temporarily hold your breath when using any sniper rifle; this helps steady the rifle until it is fired. If your heart belongs to sniper rifles, then

LEVEL	DESCRIPTION
I	Sniper Sharpshooter.
II	Invisible to enemy Recon Aircraft while moving.
III	Hidden to player-controlled Scorestreaks.
IV	Silent movement.
Prestige 1	Kar98k Sniper Rifle & Inconspicuous Basic Training

this Division belongs to you. Mountain is also for those who enjoy stealth gameplay. It's great for S&D and very effective for flanking with an SMG.

EXPEDITIONARY

The best close-range players will say that having a good close-range weapon isn't enough: you need "gap closers" to seal the deal. Use equipment as the gap closers. Tactical Equipment can be used to stun, slow and blind enemies, while Lethal Equipment can be used to cut off enemies ahead, or kill them outright. Every shotgun used while in this Division will have Incendiary Shells, which ignite enemies upon contact. It's not a huge boost in

LEVEL	DESCRIPTION
I	Shotgun Incendiary Shells.
II	Select a piece of Tactical and Lethal Equipment.
III	Throw equipment faster, further & while sprinting.
IV	Resupply equipment from killed enemies.
Prestige 1	Model 21 Shotgun & Concussed Basic Training

damage, but it adds just enough to turn the tides of battle in your favor. As you rise through the ranks, you increase the amount of Tactical and Lethal equipment, gain the ability to throw that equipment faster, further and while sprinting, and finally, gain the ability to resupply your equipment from enemies that you killed. Expeditionary excels at clearing enemies off objectives, particularly in War and Hardpoint.

HEADQUARTERS

After selecting Multiplayer at the game's Main Menu, select Play Online to enter *Call of Duty: WWII*'s online hub: Headquarters. There are several different NPCs and elements to interact with here and this section covers all of them.

STAGING AREA

The first place you see in the HQ is the Staging Area. There aren't a lot of sub-locations here, but they all have something to offer.

Quartermaster

The Quartermaster sells Collection Items and Contracts that can be purchased with Armory Credits. You can also use Armory Credits to purchase Challenges with heftier rewards than what you'd find in the Operations Bunker. To top it off, the Quartermaster also sells new clothing items, tags, emotes, weapon skins and basically anything you need for customizing your character exactly how you want.

Mail

You'll find your Daily Combat bonus, Payroll. Payroll appears once every four hours and Daily Combat bonus appears once every 24 hours. Make a point to check your mail on a regular basis to bank those Armory Points and retrieve other important parcels.

Career Leaderboard

Take a peek at this Leaderboard to see the overall stats of every player currently in the HQ and, better yet, where you rank among them.

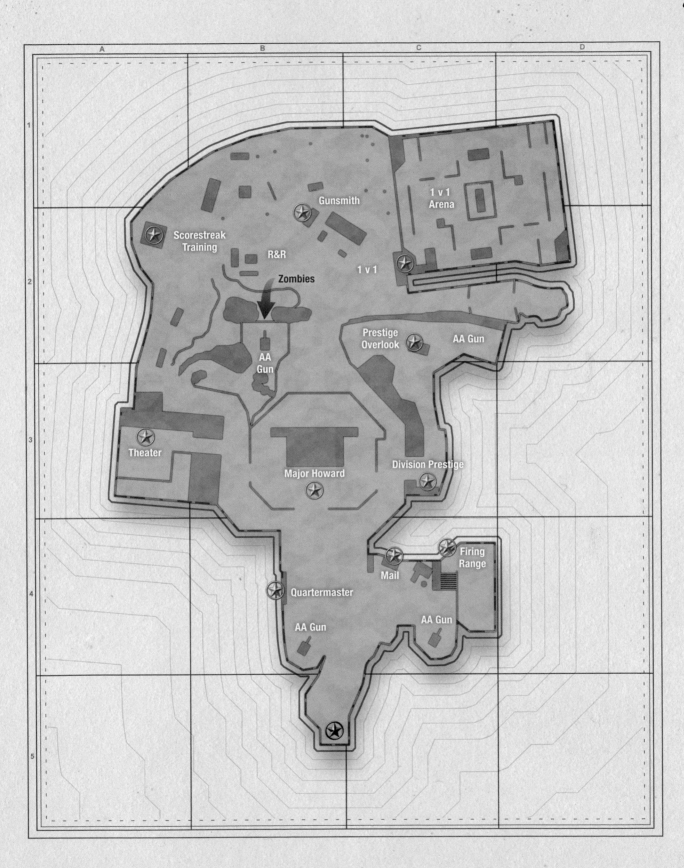

1 v 1
Arena

Gunsmith

Scorestreak
Training

R&R

1 v 1

Zombies

Prestige
Overlook

AA Gun

AA
Gun

Theater

Major Howard

Division Prestige

Firing
Range

Mail

Quartermaster

AA Gun

AA Gun

FIRING RANGE

Next, head to the right side of the Staging Area to locate the Firing Range. This is where you can test your weapons and get a general understanding of your time-to-kill with each weapon.

Shooting all of the specific type of targets can make interesting things happen. To finish the "Complete a Firing Range Sequence" Special Order from the Operations Bunker, this is the place to go.

MAJOR HOWARD

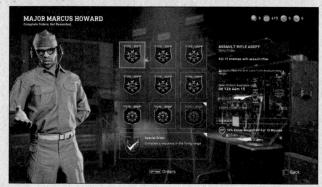

Major Howard, is where Daily, Weekly and Special Orders are found. Completing these Orders results in Supply Drops, bulk XP, temporary XP buffs, and Armory Credits. The tasks you must complete include: getting a certain number of kills during Public or Ranked Matches, receiving Commendations, obtaining a positive K/D ratio in certain Game Modes, among many others. Although it's not a requirement to complete any Orders, you'll get a lot of benefit from filling out your Orders queue and completing them.

There is a limit to the number of Orders you can have selected at one time. It's only possible to have three 24-hour Orders, three seven-day Orders, and one Special Order at a time. Make a point to select Orders that are easy to complete, so you can grab more and keep racking up rewards.

THEATER

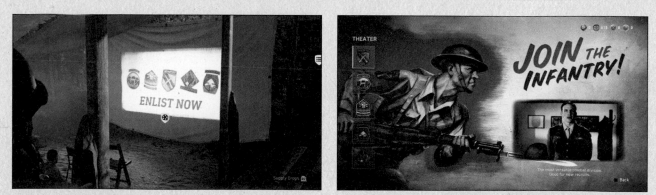

If you're looking for information on the Divisions, visit the Theater and watch the available videos. There are propaganda videos with updates and information about the game. You'll also find the Leaderboard for Ranked Play, which you can use to see your standing among your fellow soldiers in the HQ. Theater also contains "Call of Duty on MLG" where there are on-demand videos and live event streams of MLG Call of Duty matches.

THE OVERLOOK

Upon reaching Max Rank, speak to the General in the Overlook to Prestige. The player will receive all of the following rewards when they Prestige.

Level Reset

This resets your Rank back to 1 and your Rank icon changes to match the amount of times you've Prestiged. Continue to Prestige to progressively change your icons and show your dedication to the war effort.

Keep Your Progress

With Keep Your Progress, your player rank is always reset to 1. Your Weapon Levels, Division Levels, and Challenge progress are not reset.

Extra Class Slot

True to its name, select Extra Class Slot to receive an additional Class Creation slot. If five slots feels a bit too narrow, this is definitely an option to keep in mind.

Access to Prestige Rewards

You'll be granted access to Prestige-only rewards (like the Prestige icon, calling card, helmet and class slot) and Challenges when selecting this option.

Division Prestige

You won't find this option at The General, but it is in The Overlook. Look for a board to the right of the guard who typically bars your path to The General. Interact with the board to get the chance to Prestige your Division progress.

BEACH

You'll likely spend a fair amount of your HQ time on the Beach, which has several different kiosks, leaderboards, and other elements with which to interact.

1v1

When arguments can't be settled with discourse, the only other option is the most sacred of duels: 1v1. Thankfully, Headquarters has just the location to facilitate 1v1s. The 1v1 Leaderboard is located on the right side of the Beach (if the ocean is directly ahead). This is where you can enter the queue to do battle in a small obstacle course for 1v1 supremacy.

Once two players have queued on the 1v1 Leaderboard, they're taken to the Weapon Ban screen. Three weapons appear on-screen; each player must choose one weapon each to ban. The remaining weapon is the weapon both players must use during the battle. The first player to reach three kills, or the highest number of kills by the time the timer runs out, is the winner. The winner stays in the queue and appears on top of the bunker overlooking the obstacle course, ready for any and all challengers to try and dethrone him or her.

Scorestreak Training

If you're curious about how a specific Scorestreak functions, but don't want to wait to actually use it, visit the Scorestreak tower on the left side of the Beach. You can choose from a list of all available Scorestreaks and use them right away on enemy AI.

Zombies

There's a path leading deep underground at the base of the bunker in a tangled heap of rebar and shredded concrete. Talk to the soldier down there to join the fight against the undead horde. Upon doing so, you'll leave the HQ and enter the Zombies menu screen.

Gunsmith

The Gunsmith is the place to go to Prestige your weapons. Players can only Prestige their weapons if they have leveled them all the way up. Prestige 1 players can show their clan tag, while Prestige 2 players can show the number of kills they have with that weapon.

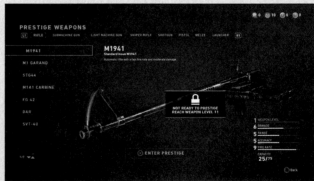

War

If you're in the mood for some War (the Game Mode, not the real deal), proceed to the War Leaderboard at bottom of the Beach. You'll also find the War rankings for every player currently in the HQ. See how you stack up with your friends and those nearby.

Domination Leaderboard

Like other Leaderboards, the Domination Leaderboard also shows the players with the highest scores for this specific game mode.

Team Deathmatch Leaderboard

You can also take a look at the Leaderboard before activating it to see which of those currently in the HQ are top of the charts and which ones are in need of more practice time.

Division Prestige Vendor

This is where you can Prestige your Division once you have leveled it up enough. Division Prestige 1 grants a unique weapon and a Basic Training. Prestige 2 grants a unique, animated calling card. Prestige 3 grants a unique uniform, while Prestige 4 grants a unique weapon variant.

HQ FLAK GUN EVENT

Every now and then, a warning will flash on-screen to alert you to an impending Axis attack on the Allied HQ. There are four AA gun emplacements scattered around the HQ; use them to fight off the attackers.

Once the cargo hits the ground, you have approximately 10 seconds to retrieve the contents. If you don't collect the cargo before time runs out, the cargo disappears. Collecting the cargo, on the other hand, results in Armory Credits for everyone who participates..

An Allied air transport will dump its cargo that Axis forces will attempt to destroy in mid-air. Hop into one of the AA gun emplacements, aim up, and fire at any aircraft with a red outline to protect the cargo until it reaches the ground.

The HQ Flak Gun Event occurs every half hour, so don't ignore it when the warning appears on-screen.

MULTIPLAYER MAPS AND MODES

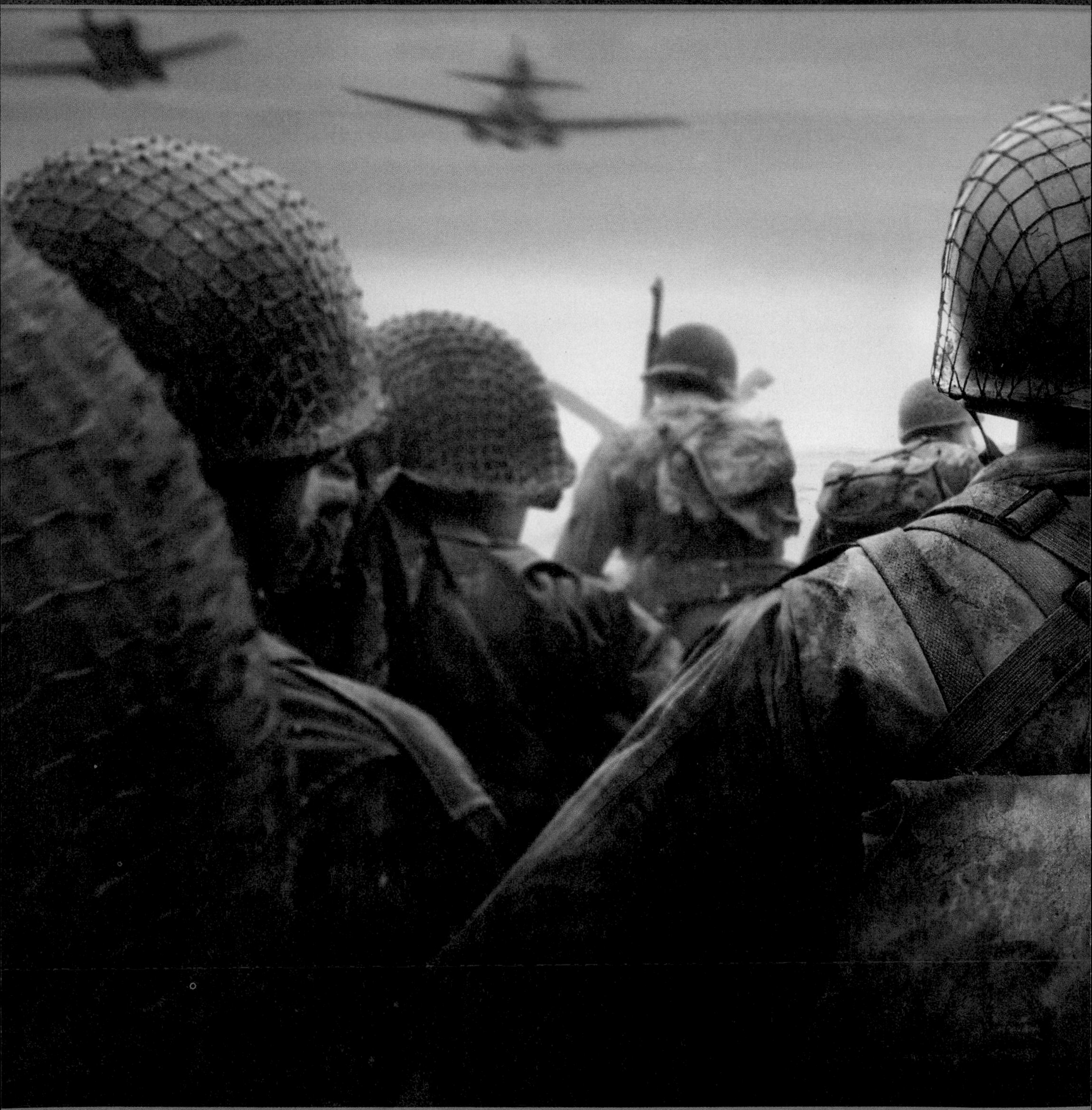

GAME MODES

There are a slew of game modes in *Call of Duty: WWII* that long-time players will recognize and a new mode called "War" that will be unfamiliar to all. Read on to get brief descriptions about each mode, then check out the maps section to get strategies and tips on how to handle objective-based modes on each map.

TEAM DEATHMATCH

Your classic team-based battle to the death. There are no tricks, frills or objectives to hold you back—just good, old-fashioned running and shooting. The first team to reach 75 points is declared the winner.

General Tactics

Success in Team Deathmatch comes down to three things: loadout, map awareness, and skill. Know your map and know your own playstyle, then use your playstyle to make the map work to your advantage. If you're a short-range player, stick to narrow, enclosed locations and stay out of open areas. If you're a long-range player, do exactly the opposite and get out under the sky. Knowing which locations on a map benefit your playstyle and which locations hamper it is key to getting the most out of each round.

WAR

War is an objective-based, constantly shifting battle meant to reenact some of World War II's most defining battles. Instead of having a single objective, every completed objective pushes the battle lines back and shifts the focus onto a new point to attack or defend. Build up walls, machine gun emplacements, and other elements of the map to help your assault or hinder your opponent's.

General Tactics

War is all about playing the objective. You won't have a lot of room to flank and outmaneuver your opponents while playing this game mode, so focus on utilizing the resources at your disposal.

Remember: it's not about kills, it's about taking your team to victory. If you cut off the enemy's ability to reach the objective, that's as good as taking down their entire team. Use buildable walls and machine gun emplacements to keep them suppressed. If they're capturing a point, sit in a covered corner and stall them until the rest of your team arrives. If the enemy has a position heavily-fortified, then spam grenades and move cautiously. You won't do your team any favors if you keep rushing toward the point and dying before getting there. Work together and think about the objective above all else and you'll have a fighting chance at taking a victory for your team.

DOMINATION

Three points appear on a map and your team's job is to capture most of them. Points tick up every few seconds based on how many control points you hold, which means capturing and holding more control points than the opposing team is the name of the game.

General Tactics

Always try to hold two points. You can go for the shut out and grab all three, but holding two points a majority of the game means you win by numbers alone. Don't get caught up trying to rack up kills; get on a point and hold it down until you see the enemy team making an attempt for a second point. If you are simply capturing points and leaving them unattended while roaming about, you're practically begging the enemy team to steal them back from you. If you have two or more points, hunker down and wait for the enemy to try and steal a point back.

HARDPOINT

Hardpoint is a battle for a constantly shifting zone. Hardpoints are captured instantly once your team stands in the zone. Every second in the zone is a point in your team's favor. If a member of the enemy team steps foot in the zone, it becomes contested and neither team scores points—at least until the enemy is removed. A Hardpoint only stays in place for 60 seconds. After that, it is relocated to another part of the map and the battle continues. Be the team with the most points, or the first to reach 250 points, to be declared the winner.

General Tactics

Learn where the Hardpoints are going to appear and how best to approach them. Each map presents Hardpoints in a slightly different way. Some have massive, room-filled Hardpoints, while others have smaller Hardpoints in open areas. We cover the locations of each Hardpoint in our coverage of each map, so read ahead and take a look at the maps we've supplied to get an idea of what you're up against before the match even begins.

This is an easy game mode to rack up a lot of points for Scorestreaks, so don't be afraid to bring some heavy hitters. Glide Bomb is a very practical and effective Scorestreak for Hardpoint. Since there's only ever one point on the map, you'll have a good idea of where most of the enemy team is located if you don't currently hold the Hardpoint. One properly placed Glide Bomb can dislodge their entire team from the point, leaving it for your team to claim.

CAPTURE THE FLAG

A staple of first-person shooters, Capture the Flag is a near endless battle (at least it can feel that way) to steal the flag from your opponent's base while protecting the flag in yours. It's stressful, it's intense, but above all it is unadulterated, adrenaline-pumping action that never gives you a moment to breath.

General Tactics

Capture the Flag is a tough mode. The chaos of battle won't protect you when you have an icon hovering over you after grabbing the flag. Use flanking paths to grab the flag, then immediately head down the nearest path with plenty of cover. You need to break line of sight above all else. It doesn't matter if the enemy team can see you with a flag icon overhead if they can't actually shoot you.

While holding the flag, you'll gain a ton of points for each kill (100 for the kill and an additional 100 for killing with the flag in your possession). Bringing beefier Scorestreaks to this mode is not a bad idea. Carpet Bombing and Fire Bombing Run are particularly devastating. If you place a Fire Bombing Run in the path of the enemy flag carrier, you can drop them and your flag along with them.

SEARCH AND DESTROY

No respawns are allowed in this attack and defend game mode. One team attempts to attack an objective, while the other tries to prevent it. This mode requires careful play, open ears, and map awareness beyond any other mode. One mistake and you're out for the round, so don't make mistakes!

General Tactics

The key to winning a match of Search and Destroy is situation awareness and loadout. Pay attention to where enemies appear on your minimap and you'll know how to approach the Bombsites and the enemy. If you're on defense, those enemy locations will direct you to an impending bomb plant. If you're on attack, those same locations indicate which Bombsite is the least defended, or where you should attempt a flank.

Keep lower-cost Scorestreaks in your loadout. Since there are no respawns, you should expect a lower kill count overall, meaning less opportunity for heavy-hitting Scorestreaks. Recon Aircraft, Counter Recon Aircraft, Supply Drop, and Glide Bomb are all cheap and effective.

KILL CONFIRMED

Kill Confirmed is Team Deathmatch with a twist. Kills are not enough to win here. When you drop an enemy, he drops a dog tag. Collect the tag and your team scores a point. If the opposing team picks up the dog tag before your team, that's a point denied. You need to make hard calls in this mode. Do you grab that one enemy's tags and score a point, or let it go to grab the three allied tags sitting nearby? Make the right calls and you'll see the Victory screen. Flounder and it is guaranteed defeat.

General Tactics

The same strategies that apply to Team Deathmatch apply to Kill Confirmed. Focus on collecting dog tags—your teammates and your enemy's—and you'll be well off. Play to the strengths of your loadout and the makeup of the map and play with more care than you would in a standard Team Deathmatch game. Getting kills means nothing if you're not grabbing tags; dying repeatedly just gives the enemy more tags to collect for themselves.

FREE-FOR-ALL

They say no one person is an island, except when playing Free-for-All, where everyone is. If you're tired of your team letting you down, and you want to show the rest of the world that there is an "I" in "team," play this mode. It's a battle to see which individual can get the most kills when there's no one around to guard your rear.

General Tactics

Stay out of open areas, but utilize windows and cover that overlooks them in order to grab kills at a distance. You're always in danger of getting shot in the back while playing this game mode, so do your best to avoid open areas whenever possible. Don't stay in one spot for long unless you're seeing a lot of action. It doesn't take a lot of kills for an enemy player to win the match, so don't sit and camp for a single kill while your opponent is gunning down foes with impunity. Ammo is a constant issue in this game mode, so Forage isn't a bad Basic Training to equip. Recon Aircrafts are also quite spectacular, since you're the only one benefitting from it.

GRIDIRON

A rousing game of football, but with a *Call of Duty* twist. You need to grab a ball at the center of the map and run it into your opponents' goal to score points. Throw it in to earn a single point, but run it in for a "touchdown" and your team will score two points. You must wield the ball carefully to succeed in this game mode. While you're holding it you can't fire a gun, but you also have guaranteed 1-hit melee kills and stronger Armor. Cleverness and map knowledge will lead you to victory above all else, so don't be afraid to try risky plays in order to take the game for your team.

General Tactics

Capture the Flag strategies apply to this game mode better than any others. The ball always starts in the center of the map and you always need to deliver it to the goal in the enemy base. Grab the ball, find the nearest path leading into a building (or other good cover) and make a run for it. If you see the goal, but you're not confident you can run it in, then throw it instead. Getting a point is better than no points.

You can't fire your weapon while holding the ball and, while that might seem like a rough proposition, keep in mind that you can throw the ball. If you see an enemy ahead while you're holding the ball, give them the ball. They'll have additional Armor, but they'll lose the ability to fire their weapon. IWhen this happens, use range to your advantage to take down your enemy. Odds are when you do this, they won't be expecting it; they'll lose a second or two just trying to figure out why their gun isn't firing, which is more than enough time for you to take them down. Grab the ball and continue on your path to the goal. Keep in mind that this won't work if there's more than one enemy ahead. If you're good, you can throw the ball to one enemy, kill the second enemy, then gun down the first one. However, that's definitely not a strategy you should rely on unless you're completely out of options.

Be willing to pass the ball to teammates and don't be afraid to retreat and take a different route. Getting tunnel vision and trying to run down an enemy will work some of the time, but will give the enemy the ball most of the time.

AACHEN

Legend ★ Spawn

🔺 S&D Plant Ⓐ Domination 🏈 Gridiron Ball 🅷🅿 Hardpoint

💣 Bomb 🚩 CTF Flag Ⓖ Gridiron Goal

A destroyed city block with interconnected, rubble-filled buildings lining its sides. Snipers rule the middle and the extreme ends of the map. Stay out of the center at all costs and focus on making the side buildings your territory and you'll do just fine.

MID-RANGE LOADOUT TACTICS

Fireplace building.

Mid-range loadouts are solid on this map, but watch out when moving through the Fireplace building. This is a short-range player's dream and a close-up fight could be over before the fight even begins. That doesn't mean you should avoid it, just don't rush through thinking a fight will immediately go in your favor.

The other side of the middle lane will be much better suited to your playstyle. The extreme ends of the map can be a challenge because of the openness and lack of cover, but with a proper rifle in hand you can challenge just about anyone, save for an adept sniper.

Church Street tram car.

The middle lane can be a real mess, so avoid spending a lot of time there. The buses are perfect for snipers and there are a solid half dozen different openings into the center, which often lead to groundbreaking levels of flanking. Use this lane to cross between buildings or for a quick flank, then get out of there.

SHORT-RANGE LOADOUT TACTICS

If you want to play with short-range loadouts, stick to the buildings lining the center lane. These areas are very friendly for close-quarters firefights, so you'll feel right at home while in them. Spend as little

Elevator room.

time as possible on the extreme ends of the map and stay out of that center lane; you'll have a good run of it if you do.

LONG-RANGE LOADOUT TACTICS

Church Street tram car.

Theatre Street tram car.

The buses bookending the center line are tailor made for you and your kind. Use them to catch any poor sap foolish or desperate enough to trek into the center of the map, but be ready for counter-snipers in or around the bus on the other side of the map.

Northwest corner of Theatre Street.

The extreme ends of the map are also very well suited to a long-range loadout. Plenty of open, flat space in the center of both of these areas will make anyone running through them an

Southwest side of Church Street.

easy target. The long alleys and buildings with cover will provide plenty of protection to fire from. Don't expect to see a lot of action in these areas, but on the rare occasion you find yourself behind enemy lines, or if enemies are pushing up on your position, retreating deeper into these areas will definitely play more into your favor than theirs.

Legend

★ Spawn

◆ S&D Plant

💣 Bomb

Ⓐ Domination

⚑ CTF Flag

🌐 Gridiron Ball

⊙ Gridiron Goal

[HP] Hardpoint

POINT A

The easiest way to reach this point is to head through the Fireplace building on the east side of the map. It's the most direct way, which will likely put you in front of a lot of enemy players, but it also has a good amount of cover that you can use to work your way up to the point. You can also try going through the west building and emerge from the Slanted Apartments, then work your way around the outside of the map. Note that this will take you right past Point B, which will no doubt be a serious point of contention.

POINT B

This point is undoubtedly going to be where a majority of fights break out. It's near the center of the map and is largely exposed, but surrounded by sections of the building that provide a nice bit of cover for either team. Flank from the middle of the map to catch the enemy team unaware. You can jump into the window on either side (one leading to the Bakery and one leading to the Elevator Room) for a sneak attack, but expect the enemy to be ready for it.

POINT C

This is a challenging point to take. It's in an elevated position in a mostly open area. Anyone using long-range weapons will shoot you from a mile away. To help mitigate that, use the east building and emerge from the Bookstore Apartments. You'll be below the point's hill and can slowly crawl up to it without fear of getting sniped. You can make the capture from behind the charred bench, which will keep you from getting exposed to sniper fire. Although it won't give you a chance to fight back if anyone runs up to defend the point, it will prevent you from being a target the moment you step foot on the point. Smoke grenades on the flag can also keep enemies from drawing a bead on you.

Legend

⭐ Spawn

🔺 S&D Plant

🍎 Bomb

Ⓐ Domination

🚩 CTF Flag

✪ Gridiron Ball

Ⓖ Gridiron Goal

HP Hardpoint

TANK HILL ALLIES HARDPOINT

This point is in the middle of the western building. It's largely exposed and has very little cover. Expect flanks coming up from the middle and make a point to use them if the Hardpoint isn't in your possession. If you have a mid or long-range weapon, you can stand in the opposite building in Tank Hill Axis and pick off enemies as they approach the point.

MAIN STREET HARDPOINT

This Hardpoint is a sniper's dream. It's on the Axis end of Main Street (the middle lane of the map) and is mostly exposed to the tramcar at the opposite end of the map. If enemies are on the Hardpoint, the obvious solution is to use a mid or long-range weapon from the other end of Main Street to pick them off one at a time.

If you're on the point, hide behind the trucks in the area. It's the best cover in this section. Having a teammate counter-snipe from the tramcar near the point will help tremendously. If you're behind the truck on the west side of Main Street, watch for attacks coming from the Bookstore on the east side of the map. If you're behind the truck on the east side of Main Street, keep your eyes on the opening leading to the Elevator Room.

CHURCH STREET HARDPOINT

This point is basically the tramcar on the south end of Main Street and little else. To hold this point, your team must be in an excellent defensive position around the area, or be in the tramcar. Being in the tramcar is basically waiting for the moment when the enemy team inevitably slides a grenade into the car. If the enemy team has broken their way into the area, you can also use the sandbags in front of the tramcar for cover.

If you're on the attack, get a grenade into the tramcar. There's a high probability that at least one enemy on the point is in there. Dislodging enemies from this point isn't particularly difficult; it's the enemies hiding in the surrounding area that are the key. Try to stay on the north side of the tramcar at all times to avoid getting sniped by any hidden foes.

TANK HILL AXIS HARDPOINT

This is perhaps the worst point to capture and hold on this map. There's very little cover and it only guards you from one angle. Don't focus on winning this Hardpoint so much as preventing the enemy team from having it. Contest it with everything you've got and constantly pepper it with grenades and Scorestreaks. Scoring any points on this Hardpoint should be considered a victory, but preventing the enemy team from scoring is like winning the war.

Legend — Spawn · S&D Plant · Domination · Gridiron Ball · Hardpoint · Bomb · CTF Flag · Gridiron Goal

This is a very straightforward CTF map, but that doesn't make it easy—not by a long shot. There's basically one safe path back to your base, regardless of which team, and that's straight through the nearest building. Going up the center of the map is madness, although madness is sometimes the secret spice of success.

SEARCH & DESTROY MAP

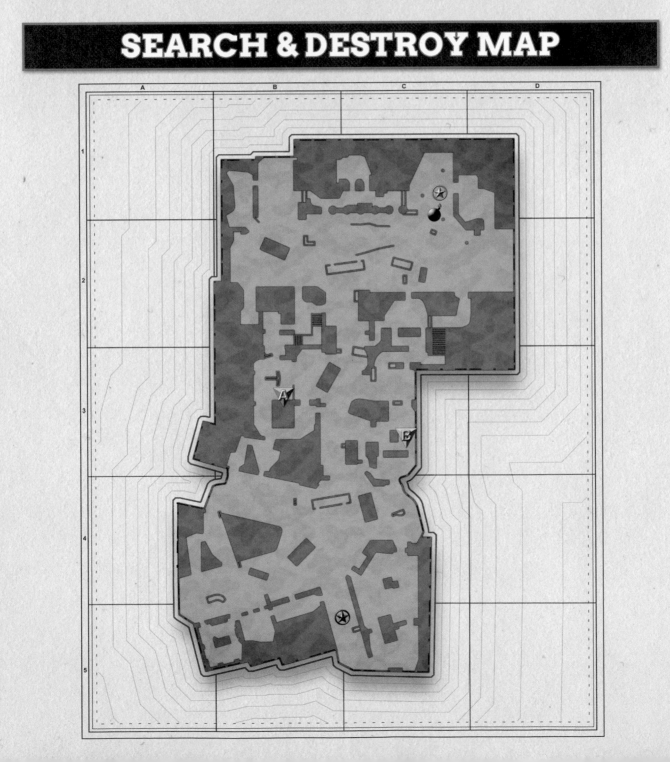

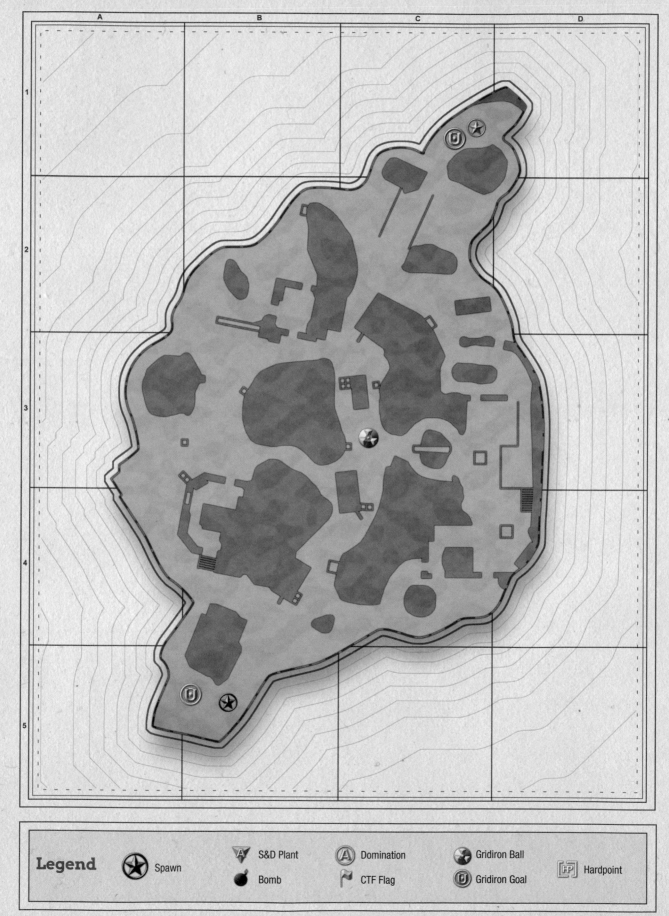

Legend ⬤ Spawn 🔻 S&D Plant 🅐 Domination 🌐 Gridiron Ball 🆖 Hardpoint

💣 Bomb 🚩 CTF Flag 🅤 Gridiron Goal

A snowy forest scene showered in the debris and destruction of war. It's not a big map, but there are plenty of ways to flank and outmaneuver your opponents. Take care when at the extreme ends of the map. They're wide open and favor the team that spawns in them.

MID-RANGE LOADOUT TACTICS

Western side of the center lane.

Mid-ranged weapons fare very well on this map, although it's not without its tricky spots. The center lane will favor short-range players more than any others, so don't get ambushed from behind the rubbish or from the connectors to the outer areas of the map.

Bunker spawn point on the west side of the map.

The extreme ends of the map can also be dangerous, but if you're using a rifle, you should have a fair shot at challenging any enemy head-to-head. It's best if you avoid the ends of the map whenever possible, as they have more favorable conditions for those who spawn in them.

SHORT-RANGE LOADOUT TACTICS

This isn't a great short-range loadout map, but there are still areas that you can fight in that will offer outs during disadvantageous combat situations and allow you to duck in close for a shotgun kill or two. Namely, the center lane of the map will be your best friend. Enter it, possess it, and make all who pass through it pay the toll. Ruins on the south side of the map also offer enough cover, provided you play it smart.

Cabin cut-through.

Eastern side of the center lane.

There are a couple of buildings and interior areas on both sides of the map and Forest (on the north side of the map) also has a couple of narrow alcoves, one on its north side and one on its southeastern side, near the cabin.

Avoid the extreme ends of the map. There are long stretches on both ends that completely lack cover and there will usually be at least one enemy hiding in them, unless your team is currently spawning there. You likely won't win exchanges here, so unless it's absolutely necessary, don't enter them at all with a short-range loadout.

Playing short-range on this map won't be easy, but you can still walk out of a kill-based game mode having supported your team if you play smart and stay away from the open areas.

LONG-RANGE LOADOUT TACTICS

Connector between the Bridge spawn point and Bridge (River).

The outside of Bunker just before Forest begins.

The extreme ends of the map play in a long-range player's favor. Lots of open space and very little cover will make these locations yours to hold. Forest (on the north side of the map) also heavily favors long-range players with open space and limited cover. You can play Ruins on the north side of the map as well, but you must be clever. You're welcome to take the overlook near the center of the ruins, but know going in that it's not hard to flank a player on that landing. Plant an S-Mine 44 below the ramp you aren't facing to avoid getting attacked from behind.

DOMINATION TACTICS

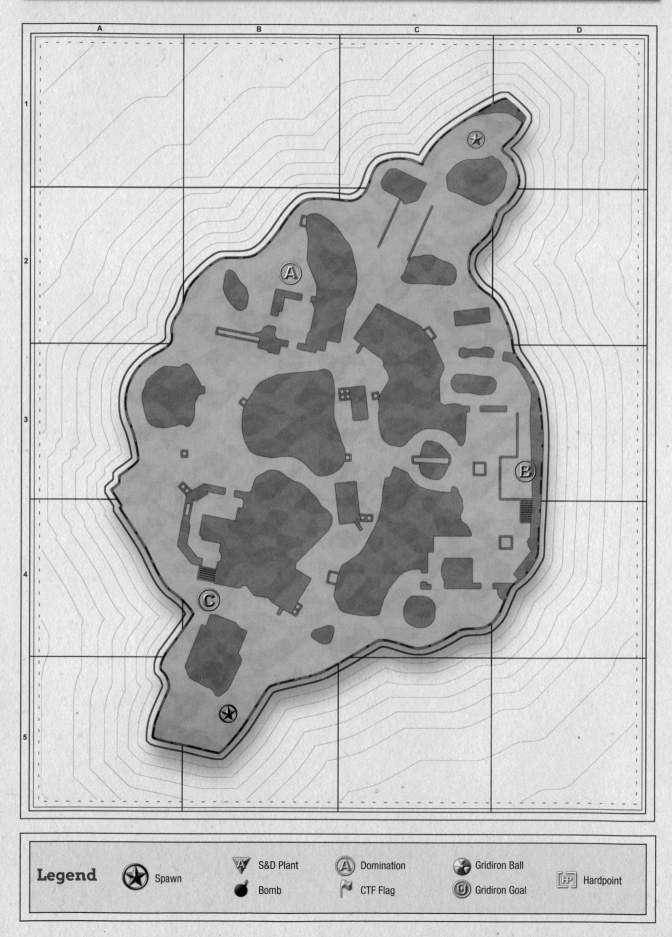

Legend

Spawn

S&D Plant

Bomb

Domination

CTF Flag

Gridiron Ball

Gridiron Goal

Hardpoint

POINT A

The unquestionable best place to attack this point is from Cabin. Trying to attack it from the east end of Forest will definitely result in a good deal of trouble. There's plenty of cover for defenders to utilize and you'll have to work around the wooden blockade, or climb on top of it. Neither one of these approaches will do much good in terms of staying alive. Enter through Cabin to gain a good sightline on most spots where the enemy team could be hiding.

If you're defending, watch for attacks coming from the eastern passage and use the cover to your advantage. Watch the Cabin like a hawk and you'll have little trouble keeping this point in your team's hands.

POINT B

You can make a quick play for this point by running up the column ramp in the aptly named Column Ramp just below the center of the map. You can jump off the top of the ramp (onto the half column ahead), then onto the point. Note that while you're trying to pull this off, you'll definitely need some luck. Remember, however, that some of the best plays are produced under similar circumstances. Once on the point, immediately go prone. You'll be exposed to everyone in the area if you're doing anything other than lying down.

If an enemy is already on the point, getting on top of the Column Ramp will almost certainly provide a clear line of sight to their position. Grenades and Scorestreaks will work nicely for dislodging them as well.

POINT C

Proceed through the center of the map or travel through the bunker next to the point to get here quickly. If you take the center, note that you'll be thoroughly exposed. You could very easily die before reaching it. The bunker is a much safer path in terms of avoiding long-range attacks, but the bunker is also likely to have enemies guarding it.

If you're the one defending the point, keep an eye on the bunker and watch for attackers coming from the south end of the point's location. You'll have a good view of the surrounding area, so you'll know they are coming well before they get there. It's the bunker that will catch you off guard; try using an S-Mine 44 somewhere in the bunker to catch anyone before they get line of sight on you.

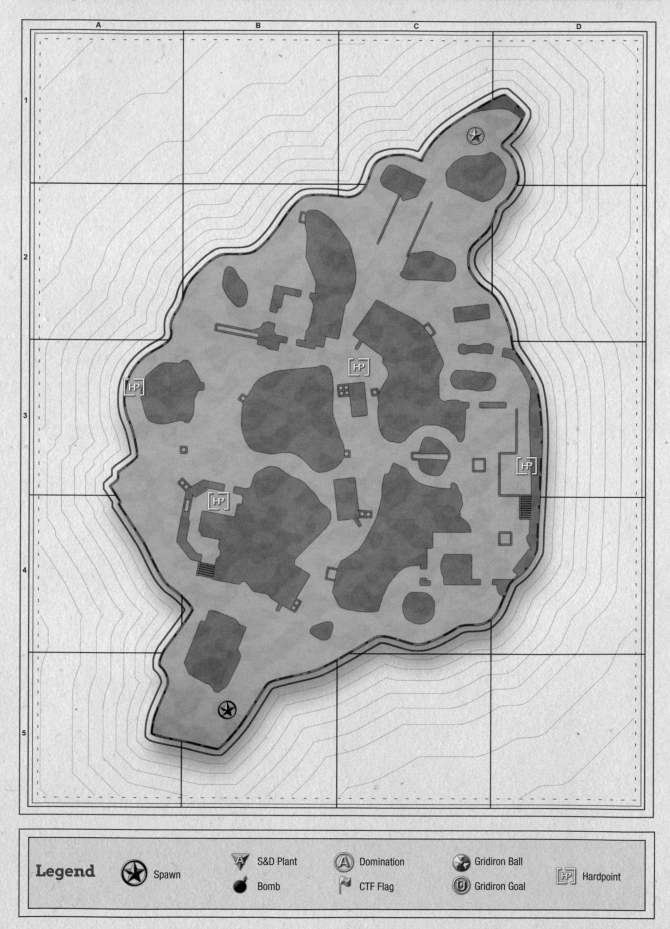

Legend

⊛ Spawn

Ⓐ S&D Plant

💣 Bomb

Ⓐ Domination

⚑ CTF Flag

🜨 Gridiron Ball

🜨 Gridiron Goal

HP Hardpoint

CAVE HARDPOINT

This point is one big kill box for whoever is in it. There's no cover in the Cave and the only way to avoid getting shot from a long distance is to move toward the other side of Cave. Therein lies the problem: moving to either side of Cave may protect you from potential attacks on one end, but will completely expose you on the other end. Your best bet for holding this Hardpoint is to use smoke grenade on the entrances (one end will suffice if that's all you have) and lay down suppressing fire on the other side.

If you're trying to dislodge defenders, just stand a fair distance away and look into Cave with a scoped weapon. You're nearly guaranteed to see at least one player on the Hardpoint. Grenades work quite well for dealing with multiple enemies.

RUINS HARDPOINT

Go prone on top of the elevated platform, or huddle up in one of the corners at its base. Your greatest threat will come from the Column Ramp, so keep your gun trained in that direction.

If you're attacking, approach from the Column Ramp and use grenades on the corners of the platform's base to dislodge any hiding enemies. You should be able to see anyone on top of the platform if you're at the tip of the Column Ramp. A Glide Bomb Scorestreak can also work wonders for clearing the area.

BUNKER HARDPOINT

This is a very defensible point, but its enclosed nature makes it prone to grenade attacks. Guard the doorways to lock attackers out and keep close watch on the north-facing window; it will get you killed more often than anyone would like to admit.

For attackers, get grenades into the bunker and use Scorestreaks like Molotov Cocktails and the Flamethrower to swiftly dislodge defenders.

When attacking, try to dislodge enemies from the point by aiming through the window on the North side. This small window is often overlooked as a threat and can often make the difference in retaking the hardpoint.

EAST ROAD HARDPOINT

You won't get a lot done on this Hardpoint without teammates. The Hardpoint is enclosed and there is little cover within that enclosure. If an enemy walks toward any one of the four different paths into the Hardpoint, you'll be thoroughly exposed. Holding this point will depend on your teammates' ability to watch angles you can't cover. If your team isn't in sync, this point will easily be lost.

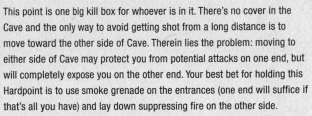

CAPTURE THE FLAG TACTICS

Legend

🟊 Spawn

🔺 S&D Plant

💣 Bomb

Ⓐ Domination

🚩 CTF Flag

🌐 Gridiron Ball

Ⓓ Gridiron Goal

[HP] Hardpoint

Both flags are in exposed, open areas but the Axis flag definitely takes the cake for being a difficult capture. If you can grab the flag and get it out of the frozen stream, you'll have a good chance of getting it home. However, the open nature of the surrounding area, in addition to the verticality provided by the bridge, make this a hard flag to steal when guarded properly.

You can reach the Allied flag with relative ease if—and it's a big if—you can dislodge defenders from both the bunker and the western corner of the map, right behind the flag. That's why it's incredibly important for Allied players to hold the bunker and have defensive positions that allow them a good view of the surrounding area.

With a flag in your possession, race it to the nearest enclosed area (Ruins if you have the Axis flag, back into the bunker for the Allies flag). Make your way toward the middle, then use that route to return to the base. Just keep your eyes peeled for flanks.

SEARCH & DESTROY MAP

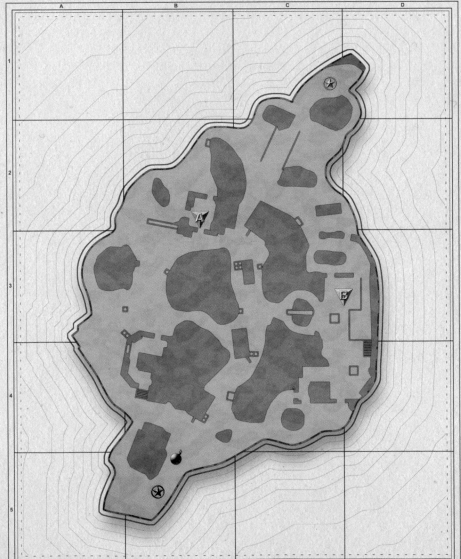

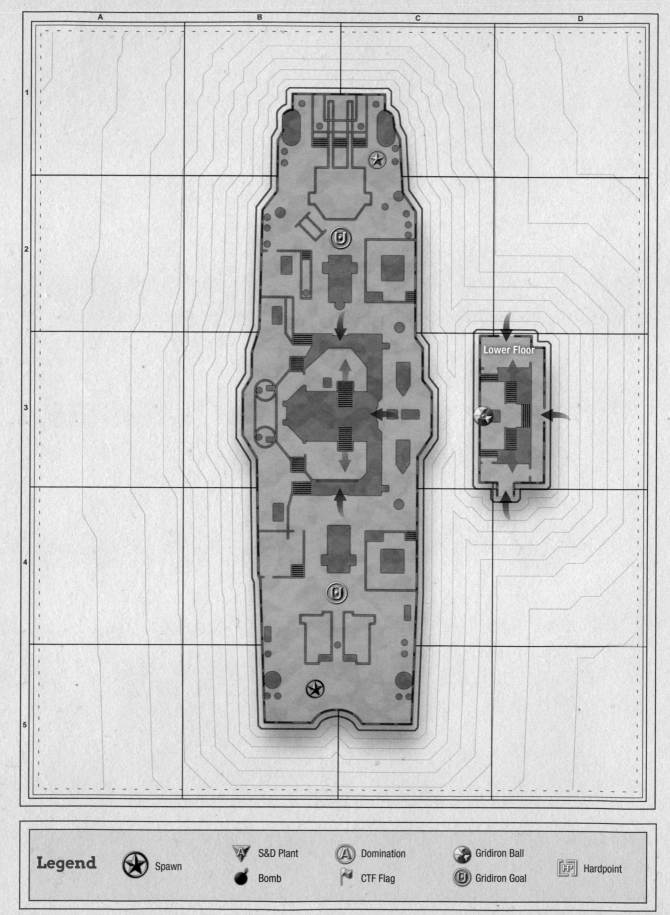

Lower Floor

Legend

⊛ Spawn

🔺 S&D Plant

💣 Bomb

Ⓐ Domination

🚩 CTF Flag

⊛ Gridiron Ball

🅙 Gridiron Goal

[HP] Hardpoint

MID-RANGE LOADOUT TACTICS

This is a mid-range, rifle map through and through. Aside from the extreme ends of the ship and its interior, you can go pretty much anywhere and not worry about getting out-ranged. Stick to cover and watch for snipers when crossing the lanes on the left and right sides of the ship. Play smart and cautiously and you'll give the enemy team a run for their money.

SHORT-RANGE LOADOUT TACTICS

Short-range is good in the ship's interior, but outside can get pretty tough. There is enough open space outdoors that trying to use a shotgun or short-range SMG to challenge enemies isn't wise. Stick to the ship's interior and make it hell for enemies to pass through it. There are plenty of routes to rotate and maneuver through to keep your opponents guessing, which even works well for melee-focused players.

Cafeteria.

LONG-RANGE LOADOUT TACTICS

Weapons Control room.

The Comms.

There are quite a few overlooks on this map, so a sniper will have plenty to do. Both side lanes of the ship have long, straight paths with great views of the surrounding areas, so make those places your home. The upper interior areas are also good for sneaking in, sniping through the windows, and then moving on. Don't stay too long up there if you want to avoid getting boxed in and attacked furiously.

Secondary Tower; the west end of the ship.

Turret; the east end of the ship.

There are two other overlooks on the extreme ends of the ship: one by the ship's cannon in the front and another underneath the ship's radio tower on the back end. You won't cover a lot of ground from these spots, but they are good for counter-sniping enemies peering through the Weapons Control Room and Comms upper interior areas. They can also be great for objective-based maps requiring a good defense.

DOMINATION TACTICS

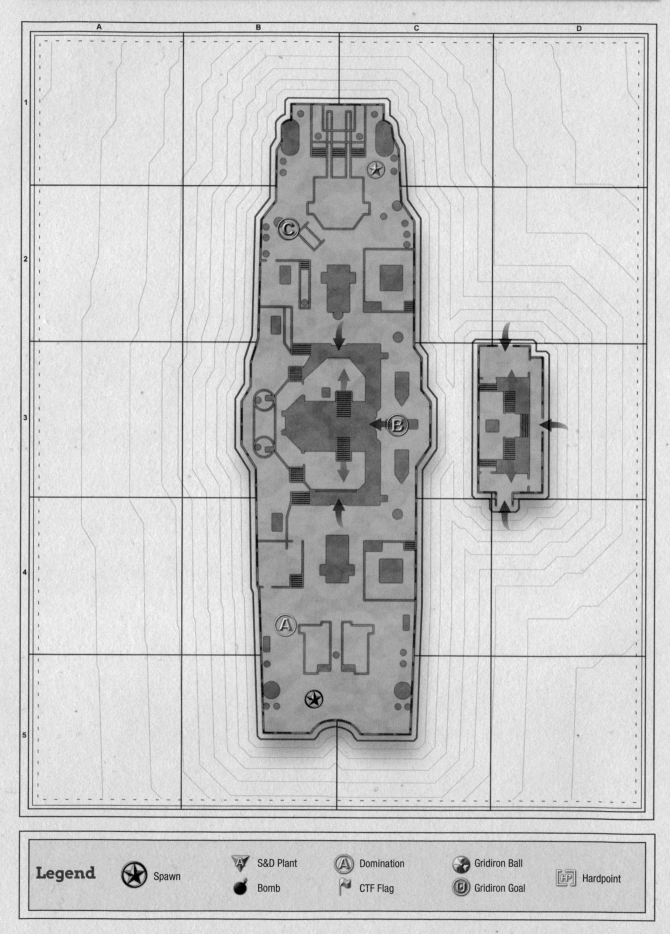

Legend

★ Spawn

🔺 S&D Plant

💣 Bomb

Ⓐ Domination

🚩 CTF Flag

🏈 Gridiron Ball

🥅 Gridiron Goal

[HP] Hardpoint

POINT A

Hunker down in the corner of Point A. Other players are almost certainly going to assume you're there, but it provides cover on your left and right. Having a Recon Aircraft makes it much easier to hold this point, since you can see them coming before you're actually in their line of sight.

POINT B

Point B is tough to capture, but the overlooks at either end of the Lifeboat Deck provide an ideal place to guard this point as a sniper. If you're capturing, watch for attacks from behind or on your sides. The door leading into the ship's interior will be on one side, while the other side is an easy path for an enemy to slip around your cover and catch you unaware.

POINT C

This is a very simple point. The lockers in front of this point provide decent cover. You can also peer down the two lanes in front of the point, which is where most attacks will come from. Stay low and play it smart. There's not much more to it than that and the same applies for attacking the point.

HARDPOINT TACTICS

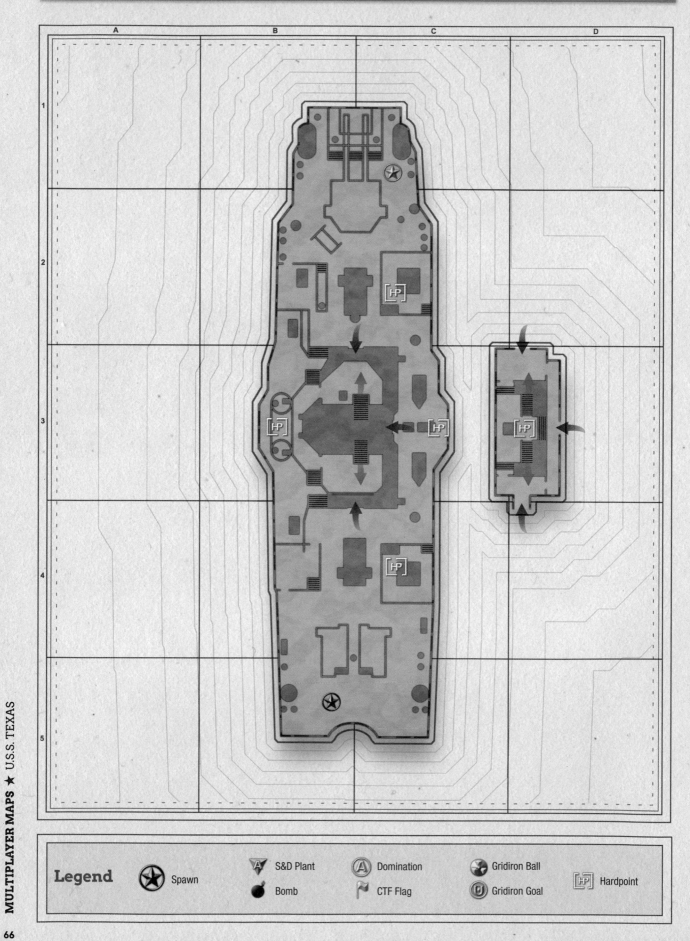

Legend	⭐ Spawn	🔻 S&D Plant	Ⓐ Domination	🌐 Gridiron Ball				
		💣 Bomb	🚩 CTF Flag	Ⓖ Gridiron Goal	[HP] Hardpoint			

MID DECK HARDPOINT

Mid Deck is a dangerous place. This flat surface, perfect for a sniper, is also seated directly below the upper deck. Enemies will pour off of the upper deck like raindrops during a thunderstorm. Use the lockers surrounding the Hardpoint as cover, as they're easily the best protection available. The object in the center of the Hardpoint provides serviceable cover, but you'll have a hard time relocating if a sniper shows up. Watch for attacks from above and stay out of sight and you'll have a good chance at holding this point down.

If you're trying to dislodge the enemy, attack from a distance with a mid or long-range weapon. Dropping in behind the defenders from the upper deck is also a great way to catch them off guard.

LIFEBOAT DECK HARDPOINT

This point appears on the side path of the ship called Lifeboat Deck, which is located between two sniping locations (albeit, exposed locations). It goes without saying to stay behind the cover in the center of the point. If you're not feeling bold, you can back off to the sniper's overlook on your side of the ship and try to support your teammates as they push the Hardpoint. Keep watch on the enemy's overlook on the opposite end of this lane and keep your eyes on the door leading into the ship if you're currently in the Hardpoint. It's a great path to take for flanking, so expect enemies to use it for that purpose.

GUN OVERLOOK HARDPOINT

The point near the front of the ship is visible from the upper level of the ship's interior, which is an excellent sniping location. You can use this location to take out enemy defenders, or force them back into a corner while your teammates move onto the point to finish the job. While on the point, go prone and block off line of sight from the upper interior areas of the ship. Although it's a terrific sniping location for your team, it can also be the source of a good deal of frustration if you're not paying attention to it.

CRANE OVERLOOK HARDPOINT

Sniper fire coming from the platform on the opposite end of the ship can help support a push on the point. Grenades and Scorestreaks (like Glide Bomb) can go a long way in dislodging enemies if they currently hold the point. You can also get a great view of the point by entering the upper level of the ship's interior and looking out its windows.

CAFETERIA HARDPOINT

This Hardpoint, which is firmly in the guts of the ship's interior, can get absolutely chaotic. If you're trying to dislodge enemies, go nuts with grenades. If you're the one on the point, try to keep cover to your back to block off line of sight and focus on the entrance. If you have a teammate on the Hardpoint, don't be afraid to step off the point and get into a corner for a safer position.

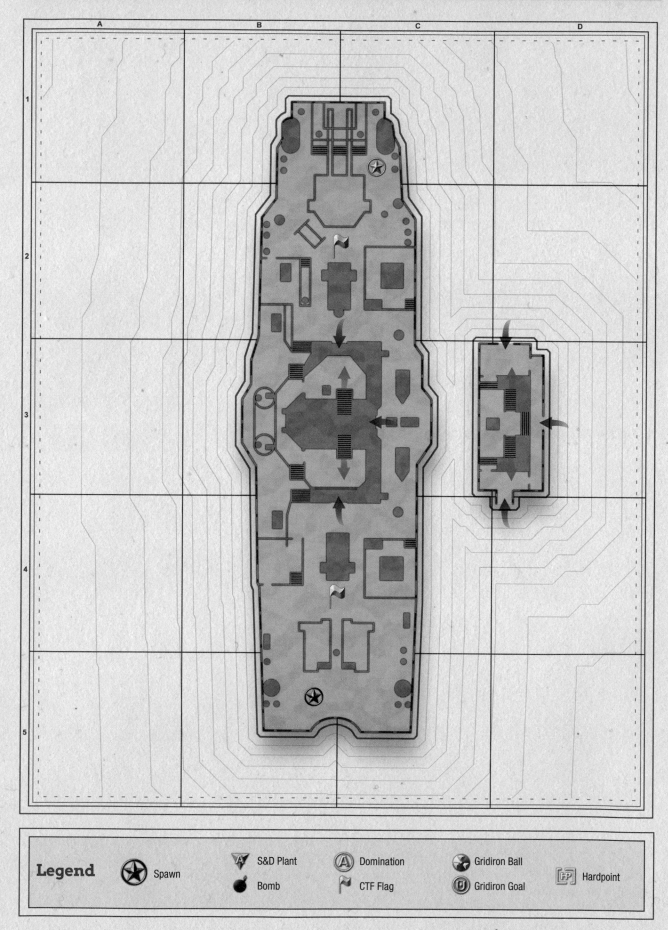

Legend

⊛ Spawn

🅰 S&D Plant

🅐 Domination

◉ Gridiron Ball

💣 Bomb

⚑ CTF Flag

🅤 Gridiron Goal

HP Hardpoint

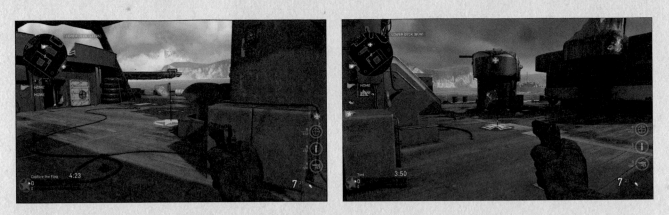

Capture the Flag on this map is a no-frills, straightforward fight to protect your flag and capture theirs. Because of the battleship's narrow design, there aren't a lot of advantageous paths to use. Your success will be determined by how well you coordinate with your team and how effectively you take out the enemy. Use the captain's room to help pin the opposing team down at their own base while your teammates make a run for the flag.

Artillery Barrage is a really effective Scorestreak for this game mode and stage when used correctly. You can use it on the enemy flag to help scatter any nearby enemies, but we suggest using it a bit behind the flag, or off to its sides. You'll kill yourself with your own Artillery Barrage if you walk into it, so placing it directly on the flag will prevent you from grabbing it.

SEARCH & DESTROY MAP

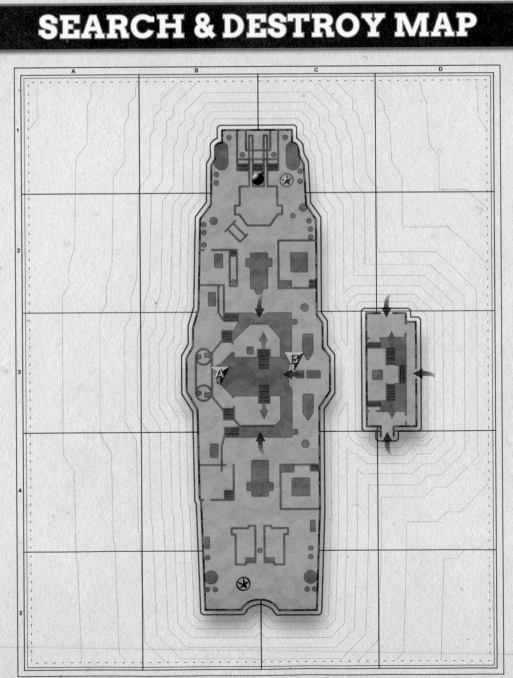

LONDON DOCKS

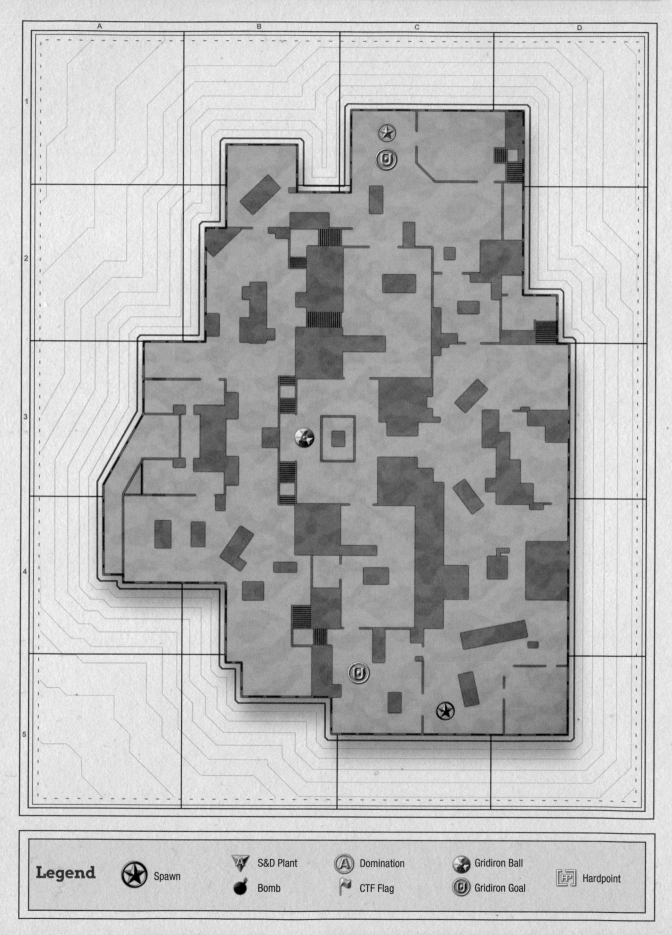

Legend

- ★ Spawn
- 💣 Bomb
- S&D Plant
- CTF Flag
- Ⓐ Domination
- Gridiron Ball
- Gridiron Goal
- Hardpoint

London Docks is a cramped map covered in crates and vehicles. It's divided into two major sections: the docks and the city block. It's not particularly friendly to long-range players, but mid and short-range players will find these conditions to their liking.

MID-RANGE LOADOUT TACTICS

The center of Main Street.

SHORT-RANGE LOADOUT TACTICS

The Wool Factory.

The cramped quarters of this map can make some areas a bit dangerous for mid-range play, but most of the map is safe. Stay sharp when moving through building interiors. There aren't a ton of locations to get flanked from, and the ones that exist are very easy to spot. However, watch out for sneak attacks coming from behind cover.

The Barrel Building.

London Docks is a map conducive to short-range loadouts. The only place that's particularly unsafe for short-range is the Docks, which is easy to get pinned down in. Subway is also a very dangerous place to visit with a shotgun, but it's a place that you'll likely only visit to get a sneak attack on the enemy team; the rest of the map is fair game. Use the cover throughout the map to sneak up on your enemies and cut off line of sight from any pursuers.

LONG-RANGE LOADOUT TACTICS

Docks Crane; southwest corner of the map.

Trains; northwest corner of the map.

This map is small and doesn't offer a lot for snipers. Your best bet is to stick to the Docks and Main Street if you're planning on sniping. Main Street is a bit cramped, but there are angles to use to gain line of sight over a good portion of the area. On the other hand, the Docks generally favor long-range play over other playstyles. While there is plenty of cover in the Docks, most of it is waist-high. This means you can snipe enemies from across the map and, even if they duck behind cover, they won't have any options to escape without putting themselves back in your view.

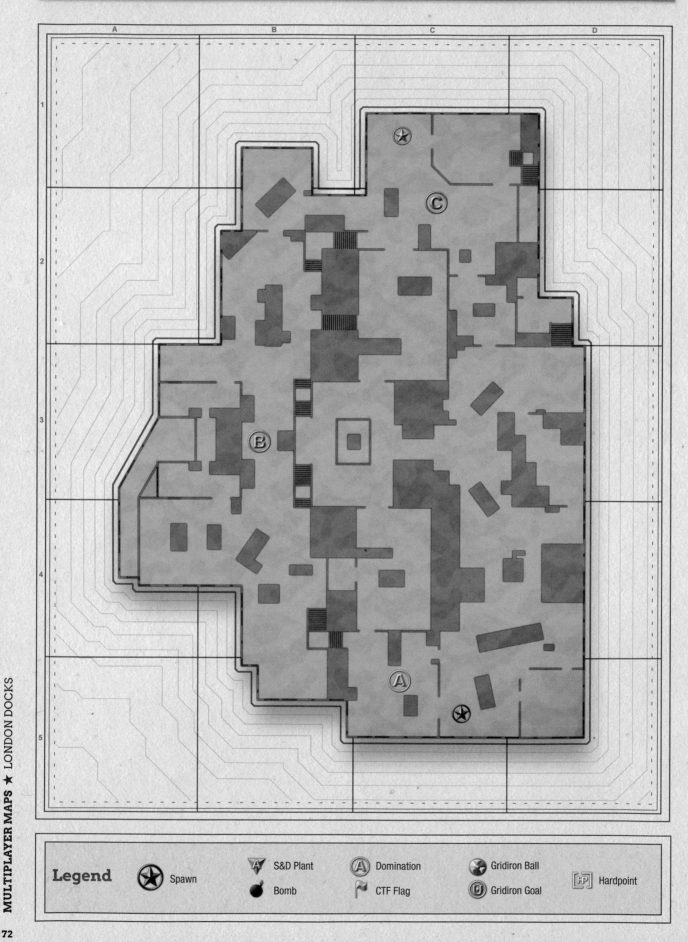

Legend

★ Spawn

S&D Plant

Bomb

Ⓐ Domination

⚑ CTF Flag

Gridiron Ball

Gridiron Goal

[HP] Hardpoint

POINT A

There aren't a lot of great defendable spots on this point. A fence and some brick walls enclose the entire location. You'll need to watch for sneak attacks coming from the fence opening leading to the Docks, but you'll be relatively safe outside of that.

While capturing the point, pick a side of the boxes closest to the point and prepare for attacks. Once the point has been captured, grab a corner and use it to defend the location.

POINT B

You'll find Point B in the center of Docks. The boxes next to the point provide decent cover, but are completely exposed to attacks from behind. You're better off huddling up against the corners of the warehouse next to the point. Watch out for attacks coming from the Statue (the plaza at the top of the stairs, adjacent to Point B), but you won't have to worry about sniper and other enemies attacking from the extreme ends of the docks.

If you're attacking defenders on the point, the Statue provides an excellent location to flank from. Even chucking a Satchel Charge or grenade will kill or scatter defenders.

POINT C

This point is completely exposed. There is very little cover and tons of ways to reach it. It's also quite easy to defend if you can take it. Just back off into the nearby tunnel while wielding a mid or long-range weapon, wait for some poor sap to try and take the point, then go in for the kill.

As for attackers, the best you can do is clear out the enemies and try to use the car (or huddle up next to the end of the wine barrels) while trying to make a play for the point. It's one that'll be extremely difficult to take alone and you will need to sweep the area clean before you attempt to take it.

HARDPOINT TACTICS

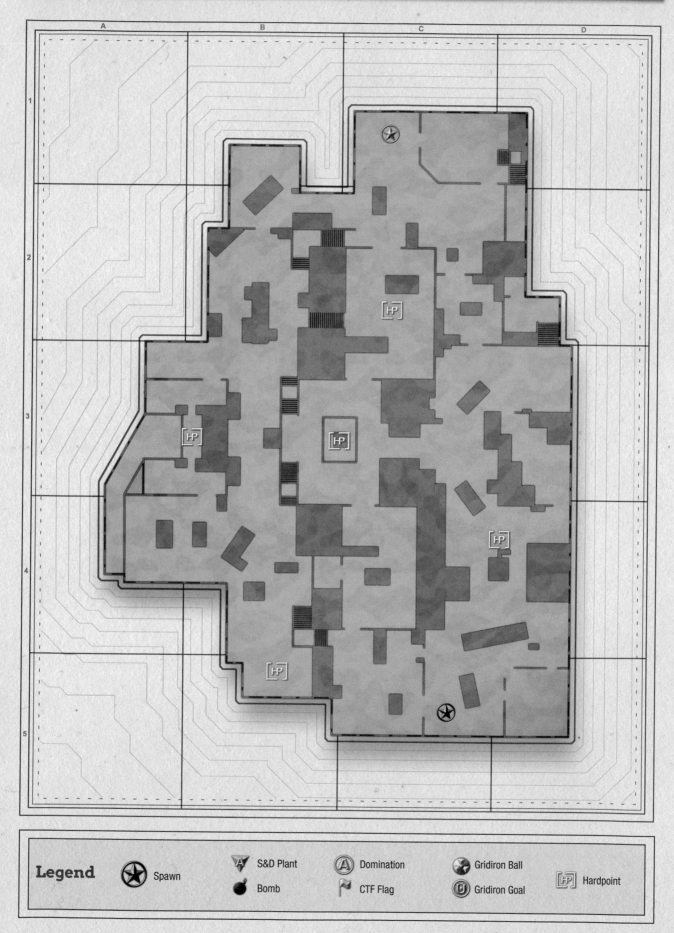

Legend

★ Spawn

S&D Plant

Bomb

Domination

CTF Flag

Gridiron Ball

Gridiron Goal

[HP] Hardpoint

STATUE HARDPOINT

This is a Hardpoint that is sure to be heavily contested due to extremely limited cover and plenty of ways to get around defenders. Use the statue for cover, rotating around it as needed. Don't expect to "win" this point. Instead, focus on keeping the enemy from scoring points on it by constantly contesting it. The Artillery Barrage, Glide Bomb, and Molotov Cocktail Scorestreaks work well for quickly clearing enemies. Grenades are also a viable option for forcing enemies off the Hardpoint.

MAIN STREET HARDPOINT

This is a very small Hardpoint with limited but serviceable cover. Expect attacks to come from the Fenced Backlot and through the Clocktower Building.

If you're on the attack, a pincer strike with teammates will leave the defenders with nowhere to hide. Coming from either side forces them to the opposite side of their cover, which will leave them completely exposed to a teammate's attacks from behind. Get some explosives on the Hardpoint before your strike and they'll be scattered with little effort.

DOCKS WAREHOUSE HARDPOINT

This is a very defensible Hardpoint given its location. You'll have a clear line of sight from the windows on either side of the warehouse, so utilize them if you're playing with a mid or long-range weapon.

Some of the platforms lining the water below the Docks Warehouse are part of the Hardpoint and they make for a great defense or contest location. Expect flanks from here, so pay close attention to it. If you're the one on the attack, hide down on the lower platform to contest the point. You don't always need to score points to win this game mode; sometimes simply preventing the enemy team from scoring points is all you need to seal the deal.

BARREL BUILDING HARDPOINT

The Barrel Building is an extremely defensible point with plenty of cover. If your team is holding the Hardpoint, use the corners for defense. You'll have little issue gunning down enemies as they enter the building while camping the corners. You won't have a difficult time avoiding grenades, provided they aren't specifically targeting your corner.

Make a point to watch the stairs leading up from the Docks. Players will use them to throw grenades directly into the room, generally causing enough chaos to throw your team out of balance.

If you're attacking, use those same stairs to get grenades into the room. Whether you're using Tactical or Lethal Equipment, any explosives that can break up an enemy formation is well worth the effort. However, don't try to take the point from these stairs. There's no cover anywhere near them, while your enemies will have plenty of protected places. Just stick to creating chaos to give your teammates attacking the other doors a fighting chance; that or make a play on those doors yourself.

DOCKS CRANE HARDPOINT

This Hardpoint is particularly small and is one of the most fortified—and least fortified—locations on this map. While you'll be largely protected from long-range attacks coming from the Docks, you'll be completely exposed to attacks coming from the opening in the Fenced Backlot's fence. If you have at least one teammate on the Hardpoint, consider climbing up to the Fenced Backlot and making a defensive stand there. If you can prevent enemies from reaching that opening in the fence your teammates will stay safe.

On the other side of the coin, hit the opening hard when attacking the Fenced Backlot. Get grenades in there with reckless abandon and serve up your own special brand of chaos.

CAPTURE THE FLAG TACTICS

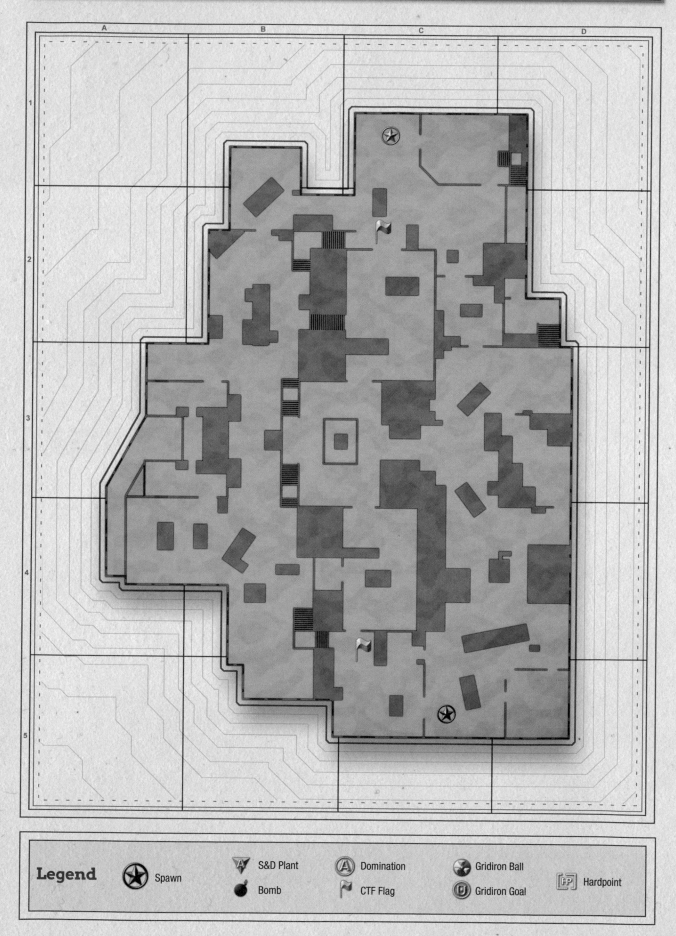

Legend

⬟ Spawn   ◹ S&D Plant   Ⓐ Domination   ◉ Gridiron Ball

💣 Bomb   ⚑ CTF Flag   Ⓖ Gridiron Goal   HP Hardpoint

This map and mode makes for strange bedfellows. Normally, the goal is to grab the flag, then flee indoors or to an area with copious amounts of cover. But in this case, that path is actually the most direct one, meaning it's also the most contested path to take. Instead of the usual "bob and weave" strategy, try unorthodox routes back to your flag. We don't suggest this every time, but it's worth a gamble now and then.

That said, it's best to avoid the Docks with the flag in your possession.. If you've managed to grab the flag and bolt for the Docks, you're simply begging to lose it. The Docks is littered with obstacles and obstructions that barely reach your waist; a sharpshooter worth their salt will shut you down from across the map.

SEARCH & DESTROY MAP

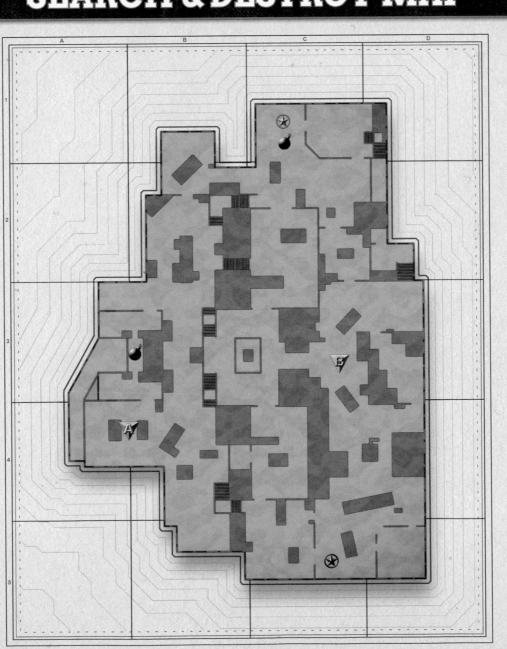

GUSTAV CANNON

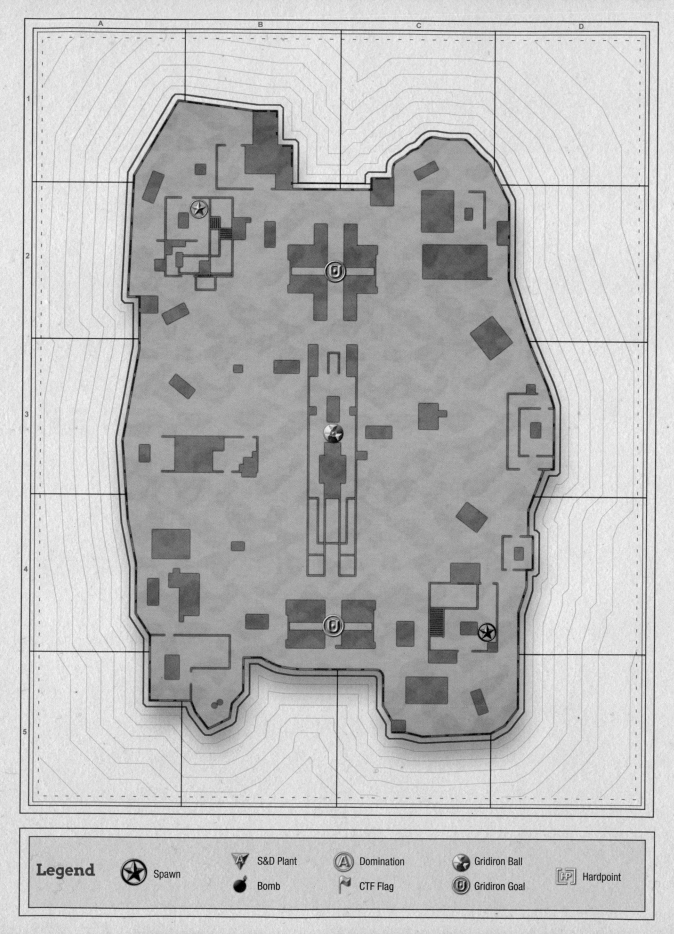

Legend

★ Spawn

🔻 S&D Plant

💣 Bomb

Ⓐ Domination

🚩 CTF Flag

🏈 Gridiron Ball

Ⓞ Gridiron Goal

[HP] Hardpoint

A small, devastated village transformed into a railway for a massive cannon called the Gustav. Those who hold the Gustav will have a marked advantage in most game modes. This map doesn't have the most favorable conditions for short-range players, but mid and long-range players will find a lot to love.

MID-RANGE LOADOUT TACTICS

Tracks North; west side of the Gustav.

Mid-range players will have the run of this map. While the open fields make for a dangerous environment for shotguns and SMGs with limited firing range, the hills and buildings are spread out perfectly for a mid-range weapon. Just avoid getting on top of the hills, running alongside the Gustav, and *never* enter the Tank Grounds. It has next to no cover, no escape routes, and is on top of a hill.

The Gustav.

The Gustav won't be your friend whether you or an enemy is on it. Although it will provide a nice overlook, mid-range weapons won't be as effective. If a particularly large cluster of enemy snipers congregate up there, it's worth trying to uproot them, but otherwise try and keep some cover between you and any line of sight a sniper might have on you.

SHORT-RANGE LOADOUT TACTICS

The view from Tank Grounds.

This map is not particularly friendly to short-range loadouts. It's mostly open with a ton of overlooks for snipers. Anyone using a weapon beyond a shotgun or pistol will have a marked advantage against you in a head-to-head fight.

Use the hills and buildings to your advantage.

If you insist on using a short-range weapon, we suggest you stay on the west side of the map. Most of the east side is open, especially Tank Grounds—*stay away from Tank Grounds!* When on the west side of the map, never go on top of the hills or alongside the cannon. Stay on the lower paths and weave in and out of the houses. If an enemy sees you at a distance, pull back and find another route. You can try to re-engage if the enemy moves in a little closer, but retreating is always an option. It's better to pull back and start the fight fresh on more favorable terms than to give the enemy another kill.

LONG-RANGE LOADOUT TACTICS

The Barn.

The Barn has a great overlook of nearly half the map and there's very little cover for enemies to hide behind, aside from the hills and a couple of tanks. If you're planning on making the Barn your home, plant an S-Mine 44 at the bottom of the stairs to fend off attackers. Make sure you keep a close watch on the Gustav, however. It's an excellent sniping spot that provides a clear view of most of the map, including the Barn's window.

The Farm.

The Farmhouse (on the opposite corner of the map) has another excellent overlook, but it's a much shorter one compared to the Barn's. You won't see nearly as much action as you would in the other locations, however, so don't plan on staying long.

Gustav's west side.

Gustav's east side.

Gustav (the cannon) is a good spot for long-range loadouts. You'll have a near-perfect view of most of the map and plenty of room to move if an enemy player gets wise to your sniping location. The biggest threats come from counter-snipers and anyone who charges up the front or back entrances of Gustav. There's plenty of cover to hide behind if you're getting counter-sniped, but there's not a lot of space for a direct firefight. If an enemy player with a mid or short-range weapon manages to get onto the Gustav, they'll almost certainly have the advantage in a firefight, so guard the Gustav as much as you revel in its bounty of sniping locations.

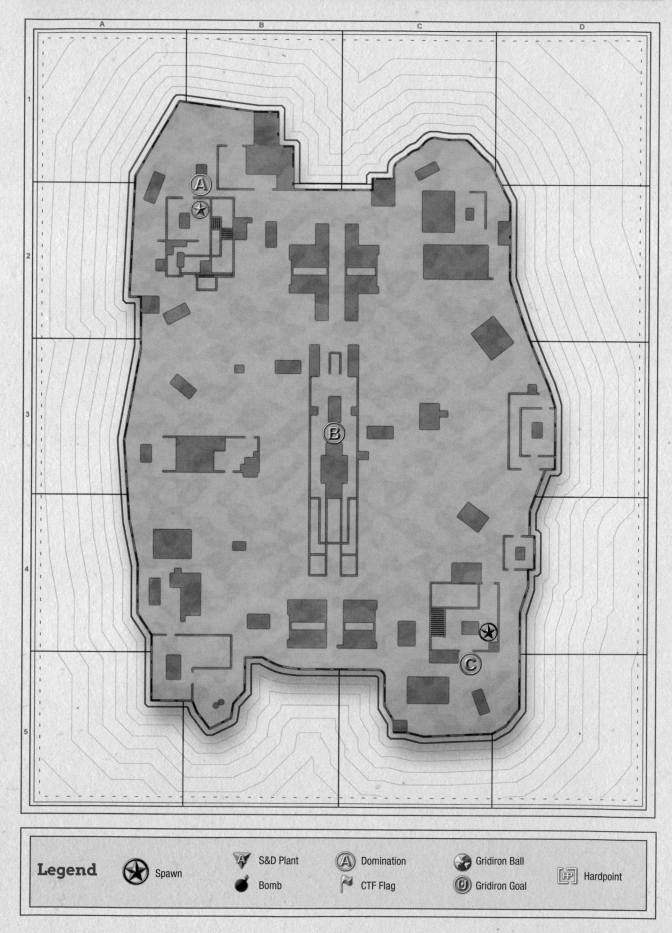

Legend

★ Spawn

🔻 S&D Plant

💣 Bomb

Ⓐ Domination

🚩 CTF Flag

Ⓐ Gridiron Ball

Ⓤ Gridiron Goal

[HP] Hardpoint

POINT A

This point is very defensible. If you stay near it, enemies will have a hard time getting close. Place an S-Mine 44 or a Satchel Charge directly on the point to make defending it that much easier. You'll want at least one teammate near the area to help you defend it, but watch out for positions that put you in the line of sight of any enemies on top of the Gustav. If you get behind cover and have a good view of the area surrounding the point, you'll have an easy time defending it.

POINT B

The major area of contention will be point B, which is placed firmly in the center of the Gustav. There are only two paths onto the Gustav and both are easily defended if you have teammates. Watch out for Scorestreaks and enemies with good grenade-throwing arms, but you'll have the upper hand when attacked directly. Of course, this rule works both ways. If the enemy team can take and entrench themselves on top of the Gustav, you'll have your work cut out for you. Use grenades and the Glide Bomb/Artillery Barrage Scorestreaks to help dislodge the enemy. If those options aren't available, you're better off trying to hold both Points A and C and ignoring Point B. While Point B is exceedingly defendable, it's just as easy to lock players up on top of it, given the lack of ways off and on it.

POINT C

The point that is closest to your starting position at the beginning of the round is the easiest to defend. There's plenty of cover here and you can use the Barn's upper floor to see enemies coming from a mile away. Watch the side paths for sneak attacks, but you'll have the upper-hand while defending this point in nearly every fight, provided you stop the sneak attacks. Take note: This map is big enough that someone will need to remain near this point at all times, or you'll risk losing it to the enemy.

HARDPOINT TACTICS

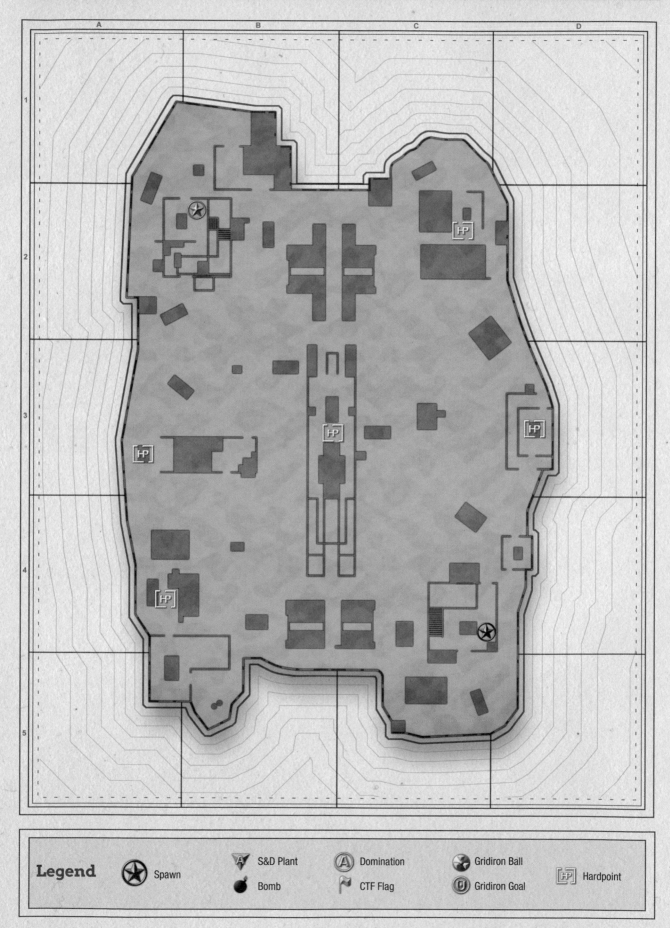

Legend

- ⊛ Spawn
- 💣 Bomb
- ◭ S&D Plant
- 🚩 CTF Flag
- Ⓐ Domination
- Ⓖ Gridiron Goal
- ◉ Gridiron Ball
- 🅿 Hardpoint

Normally, we would list all of the strategies we came up with to help you capture each point, but each and every one of the Hardpoints on this map presents a very similar structure. You'll find each one highly defensible and difficult to take if the enemy team reaches them first. The Gustav will provide little help here, too, since most of the Hardpoints have little to no exposure to the Gustav.

If you're trying to dislodge the enemy team, bring plenty of explosive firepower in the form of Lethal Equipment and Scorestreaks. Glide Bombs, Artillery Barrages, Carpet Bombers, Molotov Cocktails, and Fire Bombing Runs will all be extremely useful in getting soldiers off the point; just make sure you use them wisely.

GUSTAV HARDPOINT

MAP ROOM EXTERIOR HARDPOINT

BOMBED CHURCH HARDPOINT

APIARY FARM HARDPOINT

TRACTOR HARDPOINT

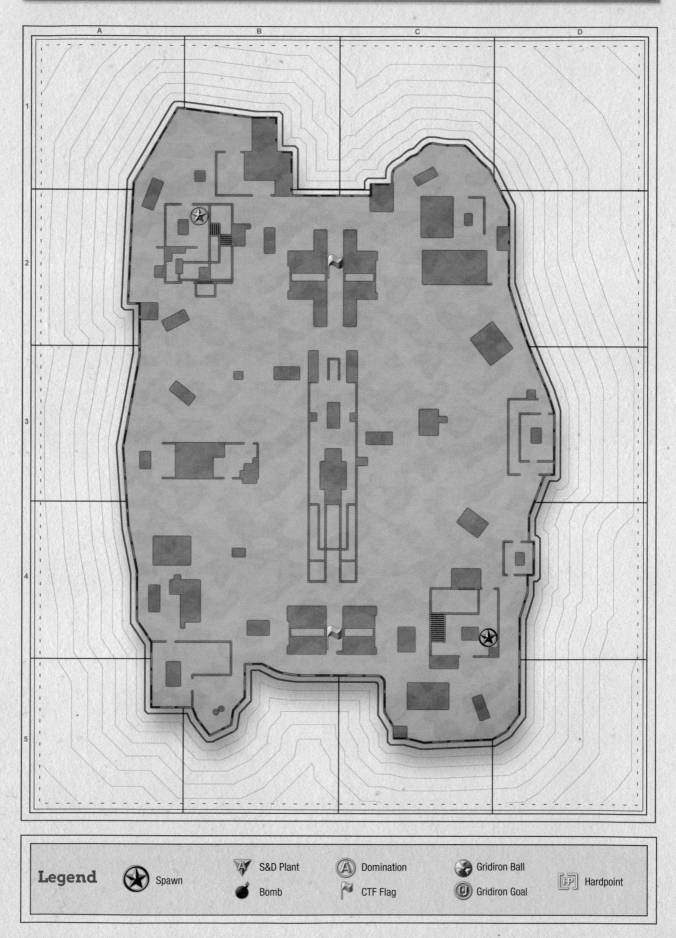

Legend

★ Spawn

S&D Plant

Bomb

Domination

CTF Flag

Gridiron Ball

Gridiron Goal

Hardpoint

The flags appear directly in front of and behind the Gustav, which makes this game mode more of a fast-paced slug out than most other maps. You can run up and over the Gustav, or go along its sides. If you do go up the side, it's best to use the eastern side through the Tank Grounds rather than the western side. There's zero cover on the western side, so if you have the flag, you'll be little more than target practice for some haute deadeye.

You can also take the long way around the outer rim of the east side of the map for a sneaky flank; or, go between the hills and houses on the west side to the same effect. Whatever you choose, you're better off making a straight line back to your base, rather than taking the same way you came in. Running up the right side of the Gustav will provide the most cover. You can also climb on top of it, but the path up to the top exposes you to pretty much any enemy who's looking for you. Once you're up and over, however, it'll be smooth sailing back to your flag.

SEARCH & DESTROY MAP

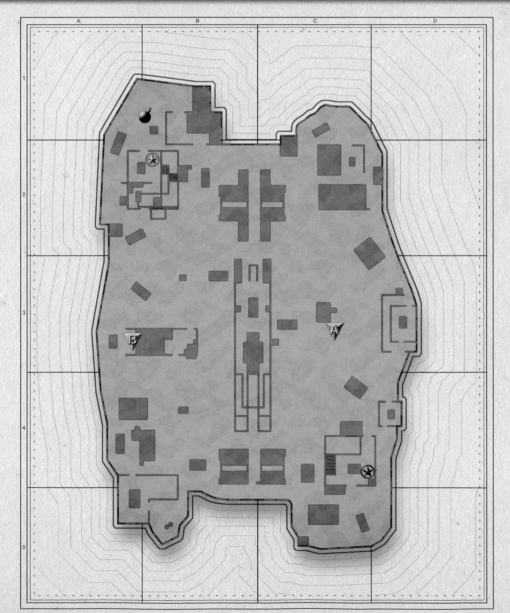

CARENTAN

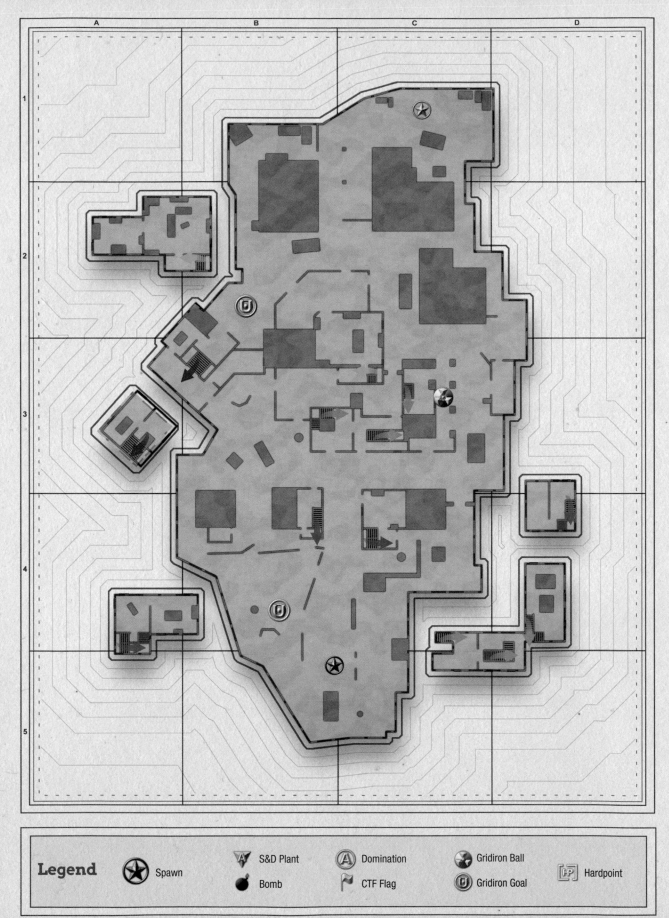

Legend ⭐ Spawn 🔺 S&D Plant 🅐 Domination 🌐 Gridiron Ball 🅷🅿 Hardpoint

💣 Bomb 🏳 CTF Flag 🅶 Gridiron Goal

Carentan, a throwback map from the original Call of Duty on PC, is a small, devastated village full of narrow alleys, second story windows and lots of sneaky shortcuts. Combat is fierce and there are very few places to hide. Stay on the move and stay alert. War is hell and combat on this map demonstrates that perfectly.

MID-RANGE LOADOUT TACTICS

Upper windows above central Cratered Street.

Upper windows above northern Cratered Street.

This map is excellent for mid-ranged weapons as much as it is for short-ranged. With a mid-ranged weapon, you'll find very few areas on the map are disadvantageous, especially with a bayonet equipped. Watch the upper windows of the ruined buildings to avoid being ambushed by sniper and shotgun users. Also, don't run straight down long roads like Cratered Street and Main Street to avoid snipers and LMG users in a prone position.

SHORT-RANGE LOADOUT TACTICS

Courtyard; center of the map.

The Tavern.

If you like short-ranged weapons, this map is going to please you. With the slew of interconnected buildings and narrow alleyways, you'll find close kills come much easier than on most other maps. Learn the interior layout of the houses and use the windows to get the drop on enemies in the streets below. Stay close to walls and avoid running the length of locations like Cratered Street and you'll find combat situations fall into your favor more often than not.

LONG-RANGE LOADOUT TACTICS

Cafe second-story window.

East end of Archway Lot.

There are a few overlooks and long alleys in Carentan, but you'll have a hard time getting a lot of use out of them—at least in kill-focused game modes. If you're going to use a sniper rifle, your best bet is to snipe while on the move. There are enough buildings that you'll never see particularly far into the map and, with the spawn points constantly shifting, you might be waiting a while for someone to pass by your location.

When sniping, stick to the long streets, stay out of houses and alleyways and don't miss. Otherwise, stick to objective-based game modes. You'll get a lot more use out of a long-range weapon when you know where the enemy is coming from.

DOMINATION TACTICS

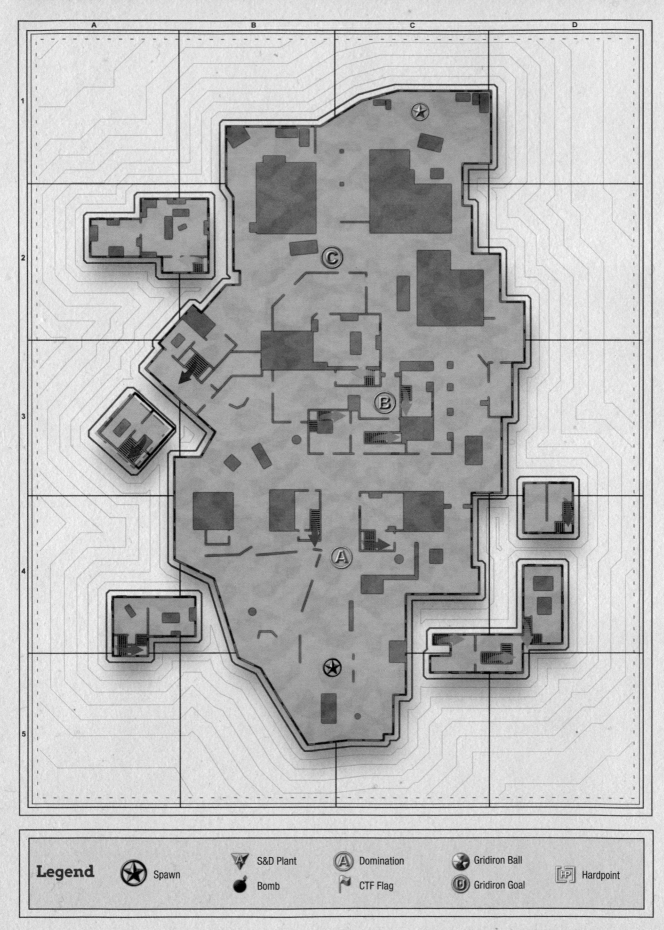

Legend

- ★ Spawn
- 🔺 S&D Plant
- 💣 Bomb
- Ⓐ Domination
- ⚑ CTF Flag
- 🌐 Gridiron Ball
- Ⓖ Gridiron Goal
- [HP] Hardpoint

POINT A

Point A is definitely the hardest of the points to capture. It's surrounded by tons of cover, overlooks, and routes in and out of it. If you're starting on Point C side, you're better off fighting for C and B, than making a hard push for A.

If you find an opportunity to grab Point A, the Café has a great overlook of most of the area surrounding the point. You can help pin down the enemy team while your teammates move in on the point. If you're going for the point on your own, try moving toward Point A around its sides. Using the Alley and the Archway Lot will narrow down the number of locations you can be attacked from while approaching the point.

If you take the Alley path, avoid the Hill and take care on the approach. There's a mounted machine gun emplacement on top of the Hill that will have little issue shredding you and your team if it's manned.

POINT B

You can see directly into Point B if you're looking through the iron fence in the Farmhouses, or if you're standing against the wall on Main Street directly west of it. If you're playing long-range, these two locations will serve you well in keeping enemies off the point. You won't be able to see all potential hiding spots, but it'll definitely help thin the herd.

POINT C

Try to hold onto the second story of Headquarters. It has a great overlook of Point C and you can very easily reach Point B if it's being taken. The windows around the building will provide plenty of visibility for most of the map and you can escape through the south window onto the Roof, then into the Apartment if things get too hot. The Apartment has a great view of almost all of Point C. If you're sniping or using an LMG, you'll have an excellent spot to hold down the point if you're looking through the second-story window.

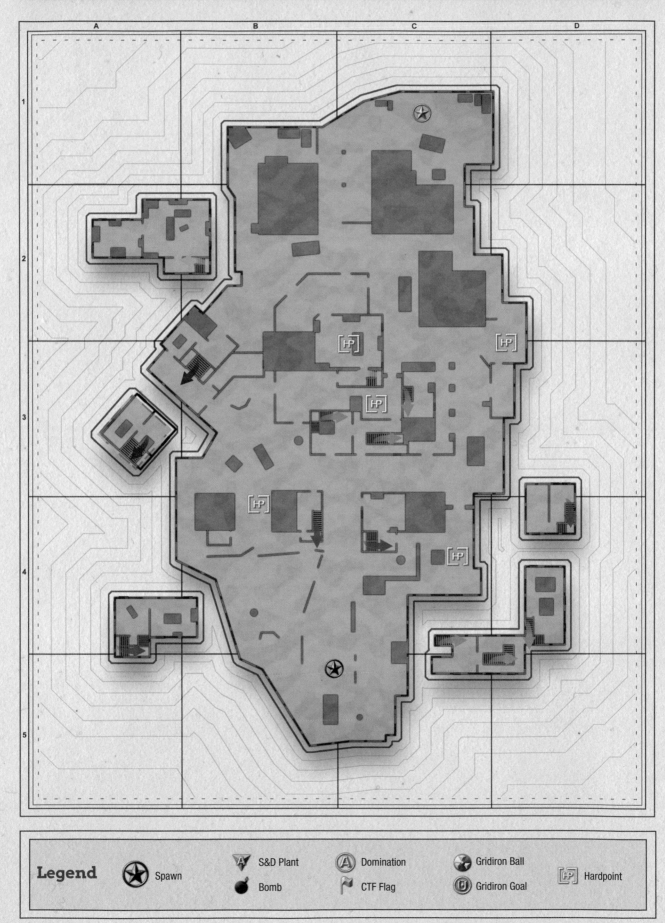

Legend

- ★ Spawn
- S&D Plant
- Bomb
- Domination
- CTF Flag
- Gridiron Ball
- Gridiron Goal
- HP Hardpoint

BACKYARD HARDPOINT

Taking the Hardpoint on this map is all about utilizing the buildings surrounding each point. When the point appears in the Backyard, use the ladder leading up to the Roof, and press up against the outer second-story wall of Headquarters. This will provide an awesome overlook of the entire point. This is great for supporting your teammates and getting rid of enemies on the Hardpoint.

If you're on the opposite side of the map, you can reach this location by entering the first floor of Headquarters and heading through the window on the second story. You'll be at a disadvantage, however, since the opposing team often spawns near the Hill, meaning you'll be completely exposed. Under those circumstances, cook a grenade, hop out onto Roof, chuck it onto the Hardpoint, and then bolt.

MAIN STREET HARDPOINT

When the Hardpoint appears at the north end of Main Street, you can use the northern second-story windows of Headquarters for a great overlook onto the point. If you're actually on the Hardpoint, use the machine gun nest to help bolster your defense. Just watch for attacks from the Headquarters windows and flanks from the Foyer's open wall and northwest Alley.

ALLEY HARDPOINT

When the Hardpoint appears in eastern Alley, using the mounted machine gun in the Apartment is a must. It has an overlook of the entire point. You'll need to watch for back attacks while on the machine gun, but you'll have the advantage otherwise.

If you need to get onto the eastern Alley Hardpoint on foot, use the opening at the southeast end of Cratered Street to get into a good flanking position. If you can get onto the machine gun nest at the top of Hill, you'll also be in a great spot to protect or dislodge defenders.

HEADQUARTERS HARDPOINT

The point on the first floor of Headquarters can be a challenge to take and hold. There are four ways in, but two of them are windows on the northern side of the room that will almost always be watched. Your best bet is to cook a grenade and toss it in, then charge in as soon as it explodes.

When your team holds this point, you can defend it effectively from the windows on the Headquarters' second floor. You'll see incoming enemies from every point if you watch the windows and the stairs.

ARCHWAY LOT HARDPOINT

When the Hardpoint is in Archway Lot, you can use the Store as a flanking location if the enemy team currently has it. You can also use the window on the second floor of the Store to guard the Hardpoint, or uproot enemies that are currently holding it.

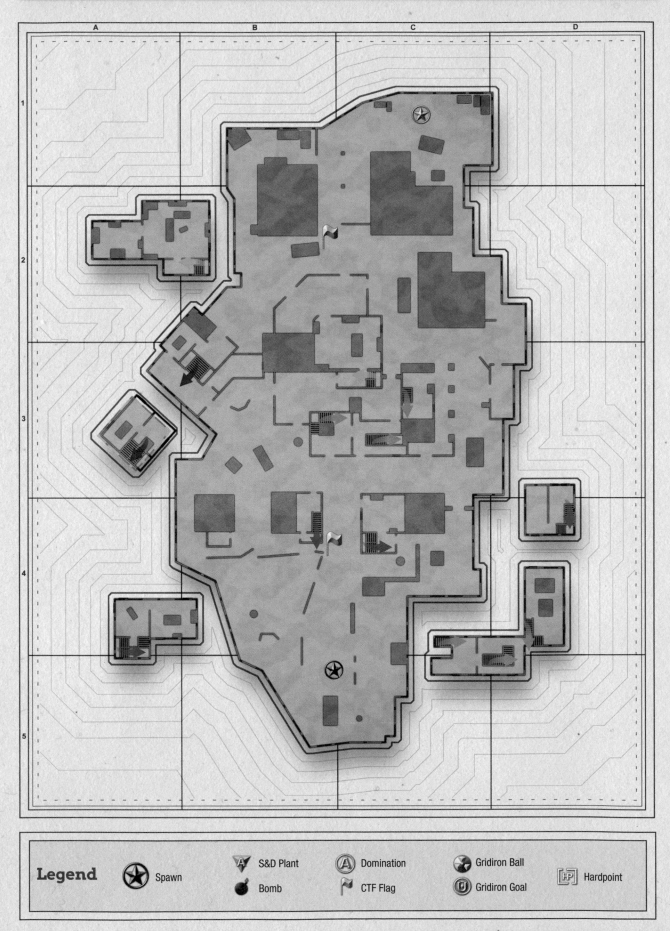

Legend

★ Spawn

S&D Plant

Bomb

Ⓐ Domination

⚑ CTF Flag

Gridiron Ball

Gridiron Goal

HP Hardpoint

Flag A is on the Access Road. It's a hard take compared to Flag B. Trying to take it by running straight down the Access Road is a great way to get killed, so stick to flanking positions. Coming from the Store, Archway Lot or the east Alley is a much better option. Plus, you'll have a better chance of holding onto it if you use these same routes to escape.

You can make a rush for the Apartment to quickly get the flag back to your base, but you'll be thoroughly exposed until you enter the building. Once inside, there's a good chance to get that flag home, but getting into the Apartment is a whole different story. Running through the Archway Lot, then taking Cratered Road while hugging its northern walls is a long trip, but a relatively safe one. Duck into the Foyer, then up the northern Alley for a good shot at bringing one home for the team.

Flag B is in the middle of Main Street and it's much easier to take and harder to defend. If can get your hands on it, you can rush back to Headquarters or the Apartment and you'll have a great shot at getting it home. The key to victory is to break the enemy line of sight as soon as you have the flag. With Flag B, it's pretty easy to accomplish that task. That's not to say that you won't have a frenzied fight back to your base, but it's a lot easier than running a straight path with zero cover after taking Flag A.

You can also use the Headquarters' upstairs windows to help support your team's flag push. You can use the Apartment's upstairs windows in a similar fashion, but it really only helps if a teammate is running the enemy flag toward the Apartment.

If you want to properly defend Flag B, it's best to hold both Headquarters and the Apartment. If you can disable the easiest escape routes for the enemy team, you'll have a much better shot at keeping them from getting far once they have the flag in hand. It also has the duel benefit of making it harder for the enemy team to chase down an ally flag carrier. Sitting on Main Street isn't the wisest move, since there are several overlooks onto the flag. Therefore, if you block off one potential enemy angle, you'll have at least one other that will favor the enemy.

SEARCH & DESTROY

FLAK TOWER

Legend
⊛ Spawn
◭ S&D Plant
● Bomb
Ⓐ Domination
⚑ CTF Flag
◉ Gridiron Ball
◎ Gridiron Goal
HP Hardpoint

Flak Tower is an anti-air emplacement with multiple paths to anywhere you want to go. Close-quarters players will feel at home here with all of the easy flanks and rotations available to your team.

MID-RANGE LOADOUT TACTICS

This map perfectly suits anyone playing with a mid-ranged loadout. There are very few open areas, but there is plenty of cover to hide behind.

SHORT-RANGE LOADOUT TACTICS

Ammo Room; northeast end of map.

Short-range loadouts are as viable here as mid-range ones. The interior locations are your safest bet, but it's also advisable to move from cover through the exterior locations. Try to avoid the center of the map if at all possible. If any enemy players stand at the windows in the buildings on either side of the map's center, you'll have a very hard time escaping.

Crane; east end of map

LONG-RANGE LOADOUT TACTICS

The Northwest Tower.

The Satellite Spawn; southwest corner of the map.

This is a tough map to play long-range. There are windows in the center of the map that might look like good sniping locations, but it's best to leave them for LMGs. If you absolutely must snipe, stick to the sides of the map. You can either fire straight down the side of the map, or try and catch an angle of the map's center for more options.

All in all, we suggest only sniping on this map if you want a challenge or are a veteran sniper. All others should stick to mid and short-range loadouts.

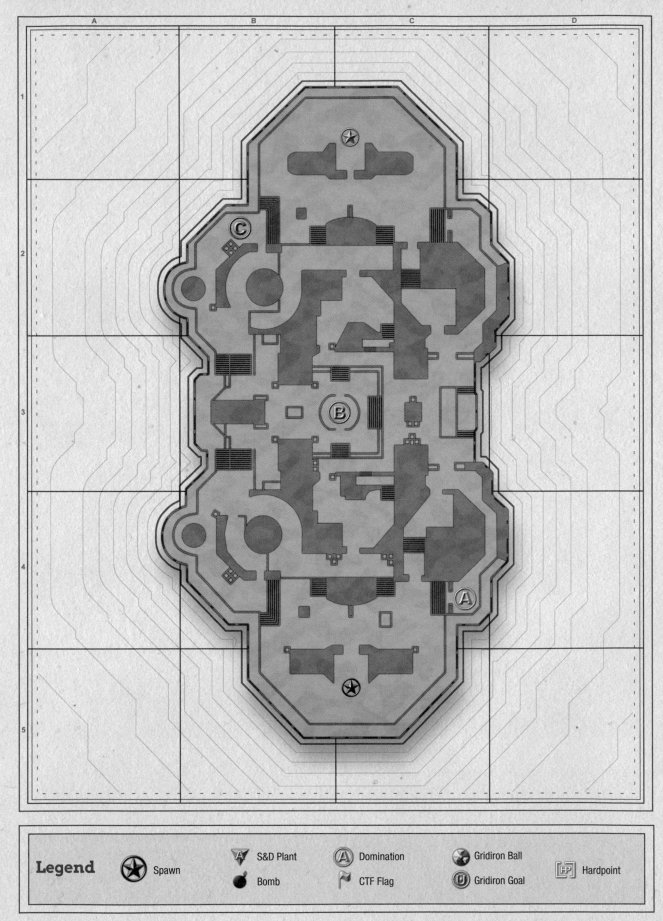

Legend

- ★ Spawn
- (S&D Plant icon) S&D Plant
- (Bomb icon) Bomb
- Ⓐ Domination
- (Flag icon) CTF Flag
- (Gridiron Ball icon) Gridiron Ball
- Ⓤ Gridiron Goal
- HP Hardpoint

POINT A

Domination on this map doesn't have any particular tricks or flanking paths that you should use over others. Its open-ended design means as long as you're moving and trying to find your way around and behind enemies, you'll have a good time. However, there are a few tricks to use to capture and defend certain points.

Point A (located at SE Lookout) is fairly boxed in. Sandbags block off the path into the southern end of the map, while it rests perfectly at the end of the narrow, east side of the map. If you're on the attack and sneak in from the north, you can go prone and set up shop with a sniper rifle or LMG to lay down some nice suppressive fire while capturing the point. It'd be unwise to stay for too long after capturing the point under these conditions, though; it will only be a matter of time before an avalanche of grenades fall on your head, or a sneaky flank comes in from behind.

POINT B

Point B at the map's center (appropriately titled Center) can be captured inside the small bunker or on top. You'll be exposed to a lot more potential fire than if you're inside, but you won't have to worry about grenades rolling at your feet. Gauge the current combat situation and make the call on which part of the point would be the best place to capture from at that moment.

POINT C

You can hold Point C at the NW Lookout by heading off slightly south from the point and using the defunct AA cannon as cover. You'll have a nice view of the greater surrounding area, which is perfect for snipers, LMGs or rifles.

HARDPOINT TACTICS

	A	B	C	D
1				
2				
3				
4				
5				

Legend

⊛ Spawn

🔻 S&D Plant

💣 Bomb

Ⓐ Domination

🚩 CTF Flag

🌐 Gridiron Ball

Ⓖ Gridiron Goal

[HP] Hardpoint

CENTER HARDPOINTS

Defending the Center Hardpoint from inside the bunker is likely your best option. Hardpoint tends to be much more chaotic than most other objective-based modes, so while it wasn't recommended for Domination, the spawns will switch up enough during this mode that it'll be hard for either team to attack with a united front. In short, everything's crazy, so hide.

SOUTHWEST TOWER HARDPOINT

Southwest Tower is likely the most difficult point to capture and hold, if for no other reason than it's heavily fortified and favors defenders. Scorestreaks and grenades will help dislodge enemies, but your best bet is to simply get there first. If that's not an option, you can try flanking by climbing up the south wall in Main Flak Gun, which will likely be your best bet if your team is attacking the other opening at the Satellite Spawn.

ELEVATOR ROOM HARDPOINT

A good option for contesting or defending the Elevator Room Hardpoint is to sit in the small room at the top of the stairs. You'll need to watch out for grenades, assuming enemies suspect your presence, but you'll effectively cut off line of sight from any attackers. As an added bonus, there's a ladder on the window's outer wall that leads right into the Hardpoint, so you can access the point with ease.

MAIN FLAK GUN HARDPOINT

Main Flak Gun is one of the easier points to contest and capture, but tough to hold. Cover is severely limited and there are plenty of ways to flank anyone on the Hardpoint. Try to stay alert, keep moving, and aim well.

If you're trying to take the Hardpoint from the enemy, attack from the north or south rather than from the center. Main Flak Gun has the most cover when facing toward the center, but barely any cover to speak of on its north and south sides.

CAPTURE THE FLAG TACTICS

Legend

⭐ Spawn

🔻 S&D Plant

💣 Bomb

Ⓐ Domination

🚩 CTF Flag

🏈 Gridiron Ball

Ⓖ Gridiron Goal

HP Hardpoint

This is a very straightforward CTF map. No frills and no cheeky paths. Good shooting skills, map awareness, and tricky flanks are the order of the day. Use Recon Aircraft whenever possible to track enemy movement, then go up the path of least resistance. Artillery Barrage is an exceptional Scorestreak for this map. You can use it to defend your own flag by aiming it directly on top of your own flag; or you can use it to pressure the enemy team away from their flag while a teammate runs for it.

Most paths back to the base are safe. Focus on breaking line of sight and keeping cover behind your back while moving. Avoid areas that have great vantage points for enemy snipers and you'll make it back just fine. The hard part is getting the flag.

SEARCH & DESTROY MAP

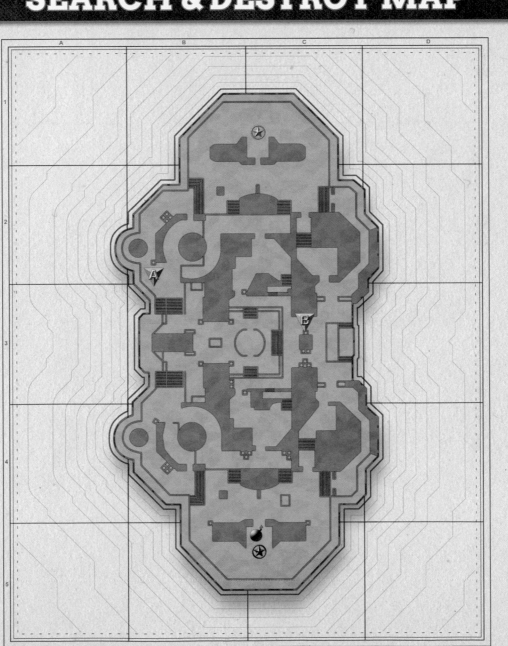

GIBRALTAR

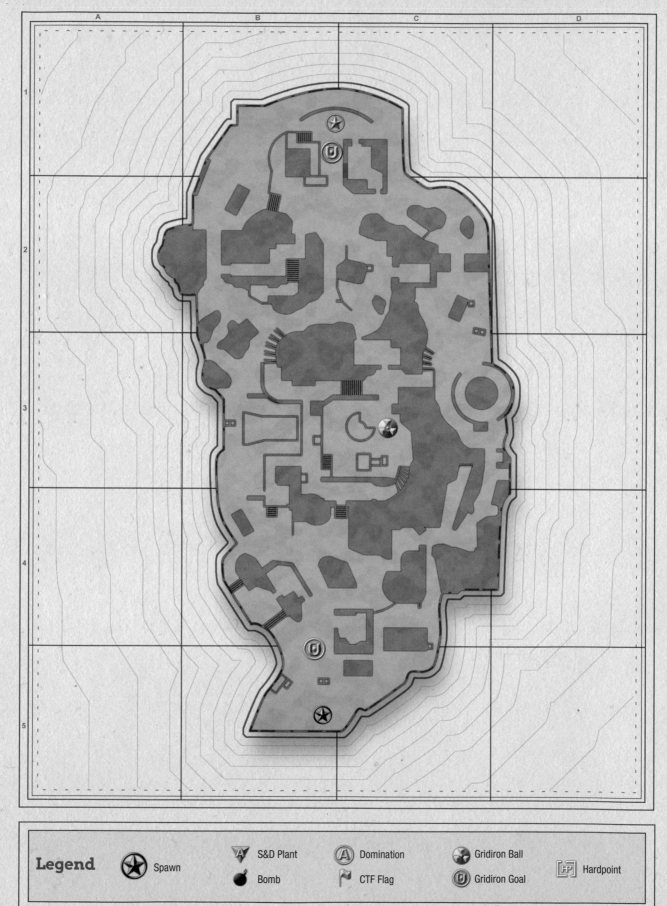

Legend

★ Spawn

⬙ S&D Plant

💣 Bomb

Ⓐ Domination

⚑ CTF Flag

Gridiron Ball

Gridiron Goal

HP Hardpoint

Gibraltar is a cliff-side military base full of flanking paths and cover with a fair bit of verticality. This map is friendly to all playstyles, but favors the creative and bold. Make clever use of the terrain and you'll run circles around your opponents or take them down at a distance before they even know what hit them.

MID-RANGE LOADOUT TACTICS

This map serves mid-range players as much as it does every other player type. Cliff Bridge and Turret can be a bit dangerous if snipers are in the local sniping spots, but you'll rarely find yourself in a disadvantageous location. Take care in the tunnels and building interiors and try to stick to the outdoor locations.

Cliff Bridge; north side of map.

SHORT-RANGE LOADOUT TACTICS

Surprisingly, short-range loadouts are completely viable on this map. The vertical nature of Gibraltar makes it easy to vault, rotate, and generally confuse your attackers. Just stay away from Turret and Cliff Bridge, as those are excellent sniping spots and absolute nightmares for short-range loadouts. Use them only to transition to new areas and never run their entire length. If an enemy sniper appears while you're running through, chances are you're as good as dead.

Cave Tunnel; southwest portion of the map.

Pit Center; center of the map.

LONG-RANGE LOADOUT TACTICS

Cave Sniper Nest; southwest corner of the map.

Fort Comms Building; east end of Turret.

Fort Rock Turret; northeast side of map.

This map is positively loaded with perfect sniping spots. The Cave Sniper Nest overlooks Turret, which is a huge open area; you'll have a clear shot of just about anyone who enters it. Place an S-Mine 44 at the entrance of Cave Sniper Nest to create a perfect, fortified location from which to snipe.

Fort Comms Building, which is stationed on the other side of Turret (directly ahead of Cave Sniper Nest), isn't quite as defensible as its counterpart, but it's still a very good spot. Expect counter snipers in one of these spots whenever you snipe from the other one.

The top of the ladder in Fort Rock Turret is a great sniping spot, too. It overlooks Fort Cliff Side, Cliff Bridge, and Castle Cliff. There is a good counter-sniping spot on the north side of the vehicle on Castle Road; use it to take down enemy snipers who have taken Fort Rock Turret.

There are plenty of other sniping spots, but the aforementioned favor sniping more than others. A good sniper will make use of most of this map, so don't be afraid to experiment and look for new angles. As an added aside, every one of these sniping locations works great as a makeshift LMG nest.

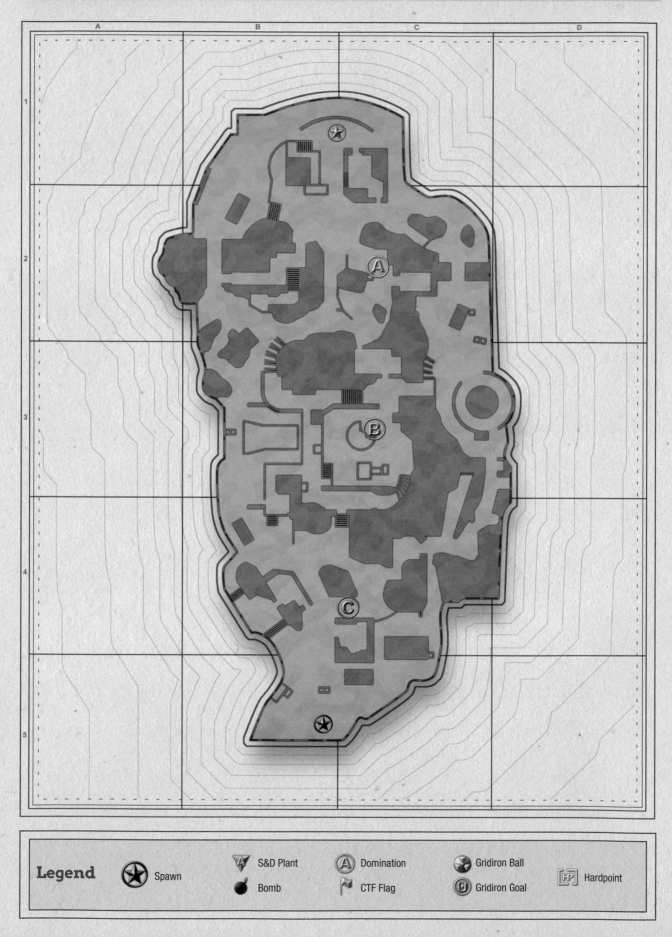

POINT A

This is a difficult Domination map. Each point has plenty of different attack routes and limited cover. M18 Smoke Grenades can help provide a break from attacks and Artillery Barrages can be used to cut off enemy routes to a specific point, which will allow you to better gauge impending attacks.

The yellow barrel in Point A makes for good cover no matter what side of the map you're coming from. Watch for flanks emerging from the Fort Comms building and use that same building if you're coming from the Point C side to take Point A. If you're on Point A and it is being taken from your team, wrap around the stone wall and flank instead of trying to charge in blindly.

POINT B

Point B is a dangerous beast. There are plenty of places to attack and be attacked from overhead or from the flank. There's not much that can be done about that. If you're coming from Point C, hug the cover to the right of the flag. If you're coming from Point A, stay close to the ladder on the flag platform in the middle of Pit Center.

This point can also be captured from on top of the flag platform, which might catch enemies approaching from Point A, but you'll be at a disadvantage if you are coming from Point A.

POINT C

Point C is easily the hardest point to take on this map. If you're trying to capture it, odds are it's in the enemy's spawn. There's very little cover, plenty of areas to get attacked from, and enemies will continuously spawn. Dropping an M18 Smoke Grenade on the point will give you a fighting chance to capture it, but even then it will be tough. Stay close to the western building and stay alert.

HARDPOINT TACTICS

PIT CENTER HARDPOINT

This Hardpoint is massive and brutal to defend. It's surrounded by high ground and there's little cover. If the point is in enemy hands, strike from the upper areas. If your team is defending the point, huddle up against the flag platform near the center of the point, as it's the safest location.

FORT COURTYARD HARDPOINT

Like in Domination, the yellow barrel is a good spot to defend from, regardless of which side you're coming from. Watch for attacks coming from Fort Comms Building, or use that building for flanks of your own when the enemy controls the point.

There are plenty of places to flank this point. Utilize them well and the defenders won't have a chance to hold the point for long.

CASTLE ROAD HARDPOINT

This point is massive and has a ton of cover. Watch for flanks, but if you huddle up in a corner or behind the vehicle in the middle of the Hardpoint, you'll cut off a lot of attacks. Watch for attacks from above and stay alert at all times to keep this one firmly in your control.

Use grenades, Scorestreaks, and attacks from above to dislodge the enemy team. It's not easy to pry this point from the hands of your opponents, but play smart and you'll have a fighting chance. Just don't run down Cliff Bridge to reach the point unless you like getting shot.

TURRET HARDPOINT

This is a brutal point to hold if anyone is in Fort Comms Building or Cave Sniper Nest. You'll be on the lowest point of one of the lowest points in the map. Stay prone, smoke the point, and keep your eyes up to shoot anyone vaulting in on the point.

If you're trying to get on the point, the aforementioned Fort Comms Building and Cave Sniper Nest provide an excellent view of the point. You can also use the connecting stairs between Pit Center and Turret as a vantage point onto the Hardpoint.

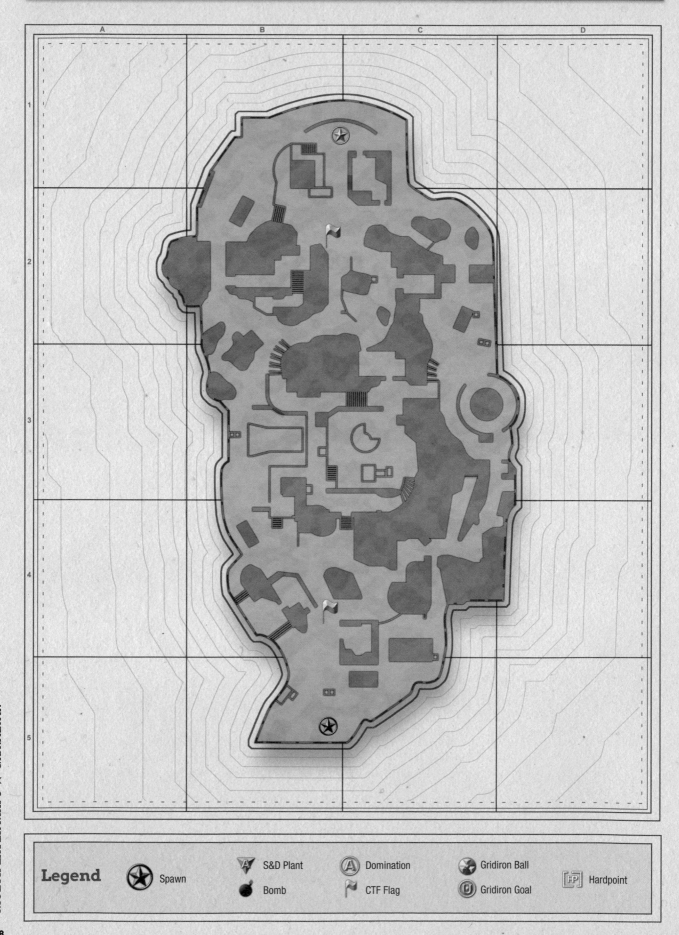

Legend ★ Spawn

S&D Plant

Bomb

Domination

CTF Flag

Gridiron Ball

Gridiron Goal

Hardpoint

There are quite a few points of entry onto the Allied flag, so stay on alert and take out enemies from a distance. The Axis flag, on the other hand, is much more secured, so those attacking must rely on flanking to catch flag guards unaware.

Stay away from Cliff Bridge if you have the enemy flag in-hand, regardless of your team. There's little cover and it's a long, flat stretch of land that will make you a prime target. It's not a bad path to take if you're approaching the Axis flag, however, especially if you use it to reach Fort Tunnel. It's okay for going after the Allied flag, but the Allies have the high ground and a fair bit of cover, so if even one player is defending that side you'll be at a huge disadvantage.

Cave Tunnel is great for reaching the Allied flag and just as good for running it back to the Axis base. If you're running through this location with the flag in your possession, make sure to jump out of the Cave Sniper Nest window instead of running the full length of the tunnel.

Don't spend a lot of time in Turret. If you jump from the Cave Sniper Nest, waste no time in getting out of the area. Any one following you can use that same window to snipe you before you can make it halfway through Turret. It's definitely not a safe place for you stay long while holding the flag.

SEARCH & DESTROY MAP

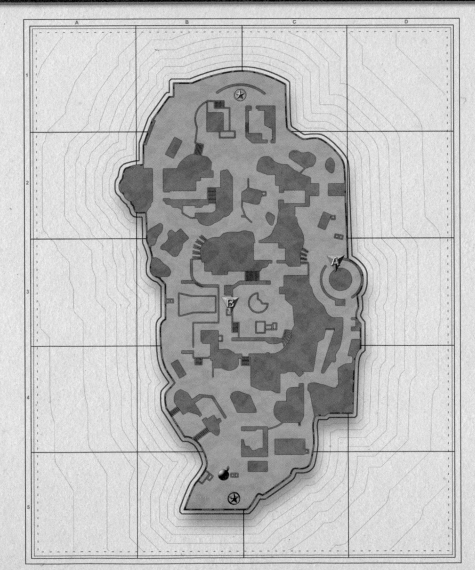

POINTE DU HOC

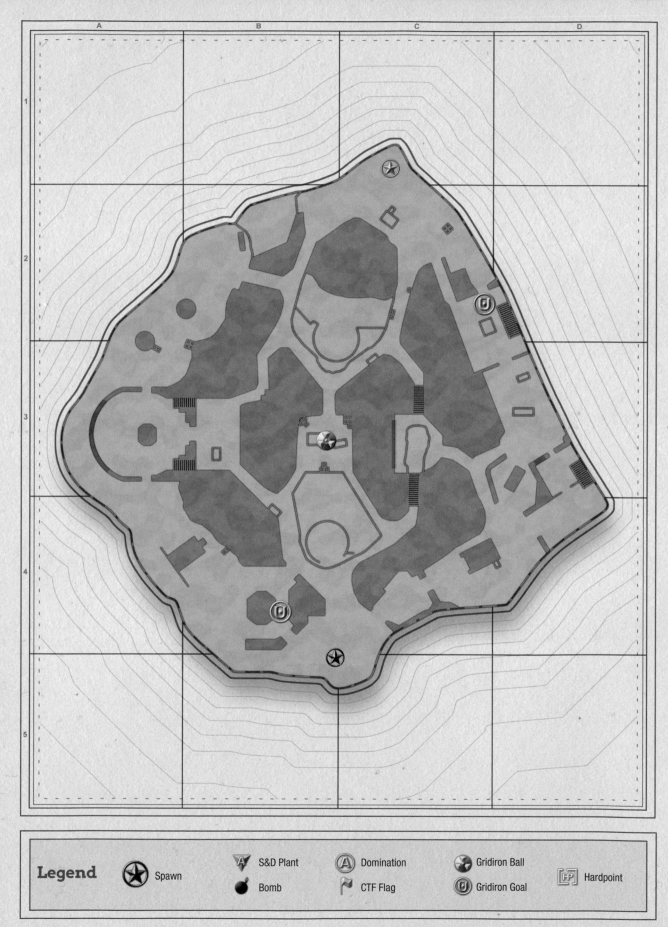

Legend ★ Spawn   🔺 S&D Plant   Ⓐ Domination   Gridiron Ball

💣 Bomb   🚩 CTF Flag   🅞 Gridiron Goal   HP Hardpoint

Pointe du Hoc is a devastated, coastal fortification with open areas surrounding enclosed trenches and bunkers. SMG and close-range players will find a lot to love on this map.

MID-RANGE LOADOUT TACTICS

Farmhouse Exterior; south end of the map.

The trenches are really dangerous for rifle users. There are plenty of flanking opportunities and enough twists and turns to allow short-range players to get in close before you have a chance to aim down your sights. Stick to the outside of the map and only go through the trenches if there are no other options. If you end up in the trenches, rely on your bayonet more than your weapon. Hip fire on most rifles isn't reliable and the time it takes to aim is about same amount of time it takes for a short-range enemy player to blast you into another dimension. Bayonets are quick and effective. Play your cards right and you'll get a lot done with a bayonet.

Most SMGs are effective on this map, especially with Quickdraw and Steady Aim as your Attachments. If an enemy gets the jump on you, fire from the hip; otherwise,

The East Trench; good for SMGs.

encounters should be dealt with in the usual fashion. There are few places on this map that don't favor SMGs: the long, coverless stretches of land, like those seen outside Farmhouse and Barn.

Tank Bunker; a good spot for the LMG bipod.

If you're using LMGs, the rules for long-range players apply in a very similar fashion. Find a spot, drop the bipod, and hold the line. There aren't a lot of paths into the buildings on the outer edges of the maps, and most buildings work well as chokepoints. If you're sporting an S-Mine 44 or are proactive in watching your flanks, you can avoid getting attacked from behind a lot easier compared to other maps.

SHORT-RANGE LOADOUT TACTICS

This is an excellent map for shotgun and melee loadouts. Short-range SMGs like the Waffe 28 perform well in the trenches, and the Airborne Division's increased stamina helps even more.

West Trench; favorable to shotguns.

The trenches are generally friendly for close-quarters fighting, but you must avoid the long, straight, and narrow parts of the trenches. If you enter a long trench and see an enemy at the opposite end, back off and reroute. There's no glory in dying in battle because you charged down an enemy who clearly had the upper hand. Playing short-range loadouts is about finesse, not slamming against enemies until they die.

Stay away from the outer edges of the maps. While they're not entirely dangerous, the conditions are not favorable to a short-range player, which will make any encounter more unpredictable than it needs to be. The bunkers are friendly, however, so don't be afraid to use them.

LONG-RANGE LOADOUT TACTICS

Barn Upstairs; southeast corner of the map.

This is not a sniper-friendly map, but there are some locations that favor long-range loadouts. You'll want to stick to East Bunker, Barn and Farmhouse as your main sniping locations. They have the best views and generally favor long-range over short-range play. Standing outside of the northwestern end of Farmhouse provides a nice view through the bunker ahead and beyond, but you'll be completely exposed. Wherever you set up shop, use S-Mine 44s to block off your rear or flanks, and then wait patiently for poor fools to pass your crosshairs.

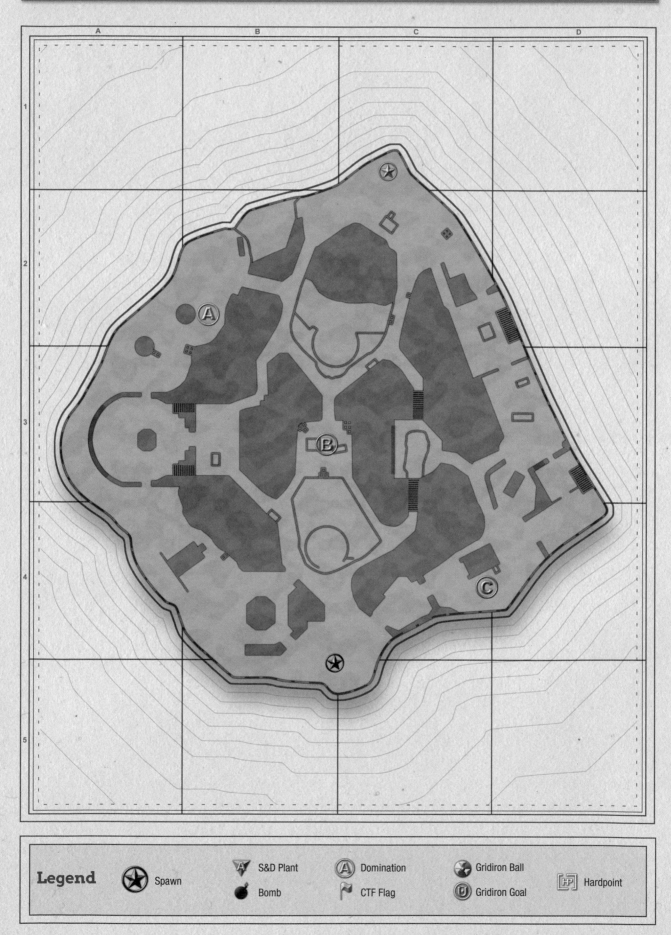

Legend

★ Spawn

🔻 S&D Plant

💣 Bomb

Ⓐ Domination

🚩 CTF Flag

Gridiron Ball

Gridiron Goal

[HP] Hardpoint

POINT A

Approaching this point from Tunnel or East Bunker is ideal, but you can also make your way around the point and use the gun emplacements as cover while maneuvering up to the point. Whatever path you choose, make sure to stay close to the gun emplacement while taking the point to protect yourself from gunfire coming from all sides.

POINT B

The more you play objective-based modes on this map, the more you'll learn about how difficult Trench Center is to defend. There isn't a lot to hide behind here; at least, not a lot that isn't easily flanked by the myriad of ways to enter this area. Your best bet is to capture the point and pick a corner from which to defend. If the point isn't in your team's possession, toss in some grenades, and try for a cheeky flank by approaching from the West Trench Battery.

Dislodging defenders off of this point isn't hard, but holding it certainly is. Success on this map and mode is almost certainly going to come down to how well you hold your starting point and your ability to take their starting point. Holding Trench Center is a consolation prize in the long run. That doesn't mean trying to take it is a bad idea, but don't sink all of your efforts into this one point.

POINT C

Don't push directly up the eastern side of Farmhouse Exterior if you can help it. There's not a lot of cover and you'll have to worry about enemies firing from the windows on the second story of Farmhouse. The northwestern side is a much safer route to take to the point because of the busted tank and the limited cover inside the house.

If you've taken the point, you can head up to the eastern second-story window and fend off pushes coming from Barn, but this is a point better defended with teammates.

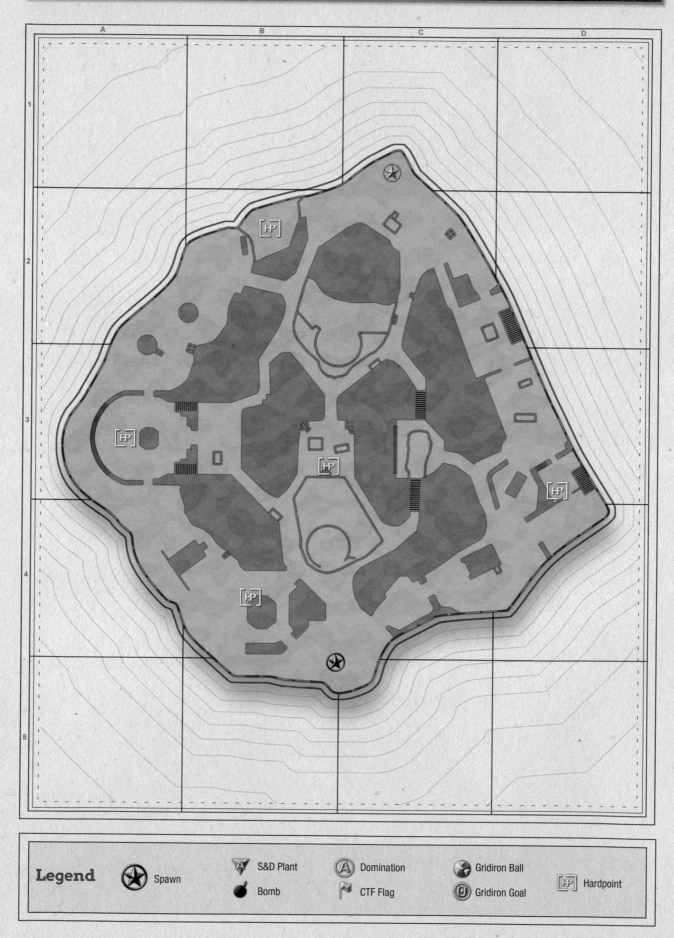

Legend

⬟ Spawn

🔺 S&D Plant

💣 Bomb

Ⓐ Domination

🚩 CTF Flag

🏈 Gridiron Ball

🏈 Gridiron Goal

[HP] Hardpoint

TRENCH CENTER HARDPOINT

The entirety of Trench Center is a Hardpoint and it's one that's excruciating to defend. There are so many points of entry, holding this point becomes an exercise in pain. One strategy to try is to hug a corner, keep an eye on the entryways, watch the bunker, and say a prayer.

If the enemy team has this point, however, dislodging them is a breeze. Use the bunkers on the north and south sides of the trenches to get a good view into Trench Center. Then go prone on top of East Trench Battery to get a clear view into the heart of the point. West Trench Battery allows for some easy flanks onto the point.

You're better off knowing that you likely won't hold this point for long chunks of time, so focus on efficiently removing defenders, then hopping on the point. You'll likely die frequently, but as long as you can get defenders out of the point quickly, you can still gain more overall points.

MAIN BUNKER HARDPOINT

The entire first floor of this rather large structure is a Hardpoint, an incredibly defensible one at that. There are only three points of entry and all of them are small doorways. There's plenty of space to avoid potential grenade spam, especially if you're up against the bunker's northern wall. As a team, cover each door with a soldier and you'll have a good chance of holding down the fort.

As an attacker, this point is likely the hardest one to dislodge defenders from. A hard push with multiple teammates will likely end in disaster, so approach this point more conservatively. Attacking from the east and west entries will provide a bit more cover than the south entrance, but not much. Smoke grenades will help tremendously, too. Getting up to the second story of the bunker won't allow you to contest the point, but it will give you a better position from which to attack. Of all the Hardpoints on the map, this is the one you want. Whoever gets here first will undoubtedly have the advantage.

FARMHOUSE HARDPOINT

The entire Farmhouse is a Hardpoint, including the second floor. There are three points of entry: one on either end of the first floor and on the ruined, northwest side of the building. The northwest side is far and away the hardest side to defend. The second floor entry is exposed and lacking in cover. The best place to defend it from is just behind the corner in the bend at the center of the room.

The northwest entry on the first floor is arguably harder to defend than the second floor. There is an incredibly limited view of the area just outside the door due, in large part, to the tank wreckage directly in front of the building.

The eastern side of the building is much easier to defend, especially if you're using the second-floor window. There's a clear view of the path leading to Farmhouse, so any potential attackers can be seen coming well before they get anywhere near the building. Because of the more favorable conditions, defenders should worry more about defending the northwest entries and have one teammate looking over the eastern, second-floor window.

If you're on the attack, the obvious route to attack is the northwest side. If they've gone light on the eastern side, you can approach Farmhouse's northwestern end, then wrap around to the building's lower east entry and try for a flank. This is a very easy point to contest, so even if the enemy team is on it, getting inside the building and preventing them from getting points is a breeze. If you can contest it, sit and wait for more teammates to arrive before trying to completely remove the enemy threat. Getting killed needlessly before you have the support to make a full sweep of the building will only benefit the enemy team.

WEST BUNKER HARDPOINT

There are three points of entry to this Hardpoint, but perhaps the most important one is on the east end. While the other two entries are small doorways that are easily defendable, the east entry is a massive rupture in the bunker's walls. You'll need to stay west of the pillar to avoid attacks coming from that direction.

If you're attacking this point, this is definitely a good spot to hit. Although with the wall forcing defenders to the west side of the pillar, you'll have a much easier time dislodging them with some well placed grenades.

EAST BUNKER HARDPOINT

This is a very defensible Hardpoint, which is great for whoever reaches and stabilizes it first. If you're one of the late ones, use Tunnel and East Trench to attack the point. Avoid using East Beach Lookout as your point of attack, however; there's a machine gun emplacement there and snipers will have little trouble using the bunker as an overlook.

As a defender, huddle up in the corner of the small overhang on the west end of the bunker. You'll be covered from potential attacks from East Beach Lookout and you can watch for attacks coming from Tunnel. As an added bonus, any enemies coming from the other end of the bunker won't immediately have line of sight and you'll be protected from grenade attacks.

CAPTURE THE FLAG TACTICS

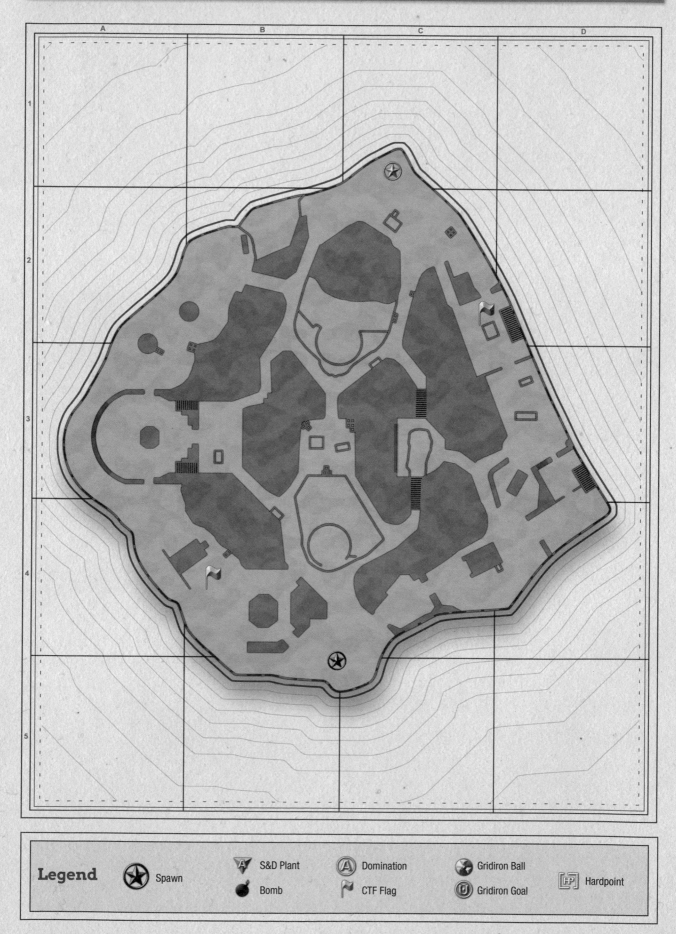

Legend

★ Spawn

🔺 S&D Plant

💣 Bomb

Ⓐ Domination

🚩 CTF Flag

🏈 Gridiron Ball

Ⓓ Gridiron Goal

HP Hardpoint

Both flags are in very defensible positions. The Allied flag has upstairs vantage points that make it hard to reach the flag building. Once an attacker has the Allied flag, they'll have some open territory to run through before they can escape into the trenches. If you're on the Axis side, clear the entire flag area before running off with the flag to avoid getting shot before reaching the trenches. If you're an Ally and your flag gets swiped, you can expect the flag carrier to run toward the trenches from the open side of Barn. Going through the front door toward Farm House is an almost guaranteed death. The average player will almost certainly go the other way, which is the way you should go as well if you're a flag carrier.

Breaking line of sight is easiest once you reach the trenches, so always make that your escape route of choice. If you grab the Axis flag, avoid going through Gun Turrets. It's a very open area with a great view for snipers and little in the way of tactical cover. The same can be said of Tank Bunker, which offers line of sight until you round the corner at the top of the hill. Grab the flag and run it to West Trenches, either straight out of West Bunker or make your way around West Cliffside and enter the trenches that way.

SEARCH & DESTROY MAP

SAINTE MARIE DU MONT

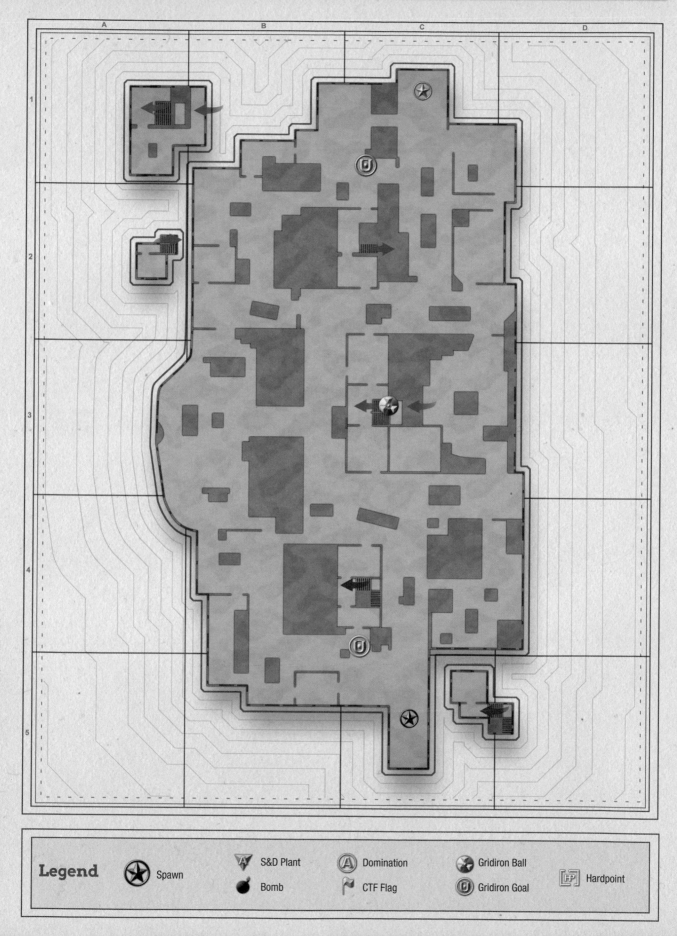

Legend
- ★ Spawn
- 🅰 S&D Plant
- 💣 Bomb
- 🅐 Domination
- 🚩 CTF Flag
- 🏈 Gridiron Ball
- 🥅 Gridiron Goal
- 🄷🄿 Hardpoint

One of the few civilian areas in the game that hasn't been completely decimated, Sainte Marie du Mont has plenty to offer for every kind of player. You'll find long stretches of coverless road cutting through the center of the map, while the outer edges are packed with close quarters and plenty of cover. This is arguably the most diverse map in the game.

LONG-RANGE LOADOUT TACTICS

Restaurant second-story window.

Farm House second-story window.

This map has very favorable conditions for long-range play. The second floor windows of Restaurant and Farm House will give you a great view of the surrounding area and plenty of cover against all but the most expert of marksmen.

Convoy Street; south end of Main Street.

Either end of Main Street will offer some great fighting locations. Stay out of buildings except to get to a second-story window and be very careful while moving through any side

Archway Street; north end of Main Street.

streets. The areas are much closer compared to the center streets, which will offer the upper hand to short and mid-ranged players.

MID-RANGE LOADOUT TACTICS

Lookout Post; west side of the map.

The long stretches of road can be dangerous even with a mid-range weapon, so steer clear of them whenever possible. Use the side streets to keep fights in your range and take care while going through buildings, as they are better suited for short-range play.

SHORT-RANGE LOADOUT TACTICS

There are plenty of areas on this map that are completely unsuited for short-range play, but those areas are by no means the rule of the day. Stay off of the streets that cut through the center of the map. Instead, stick to the side streets and buildings and you'll actually find it's completely playable with short-range weaponry.

Farm House; south end of the map.

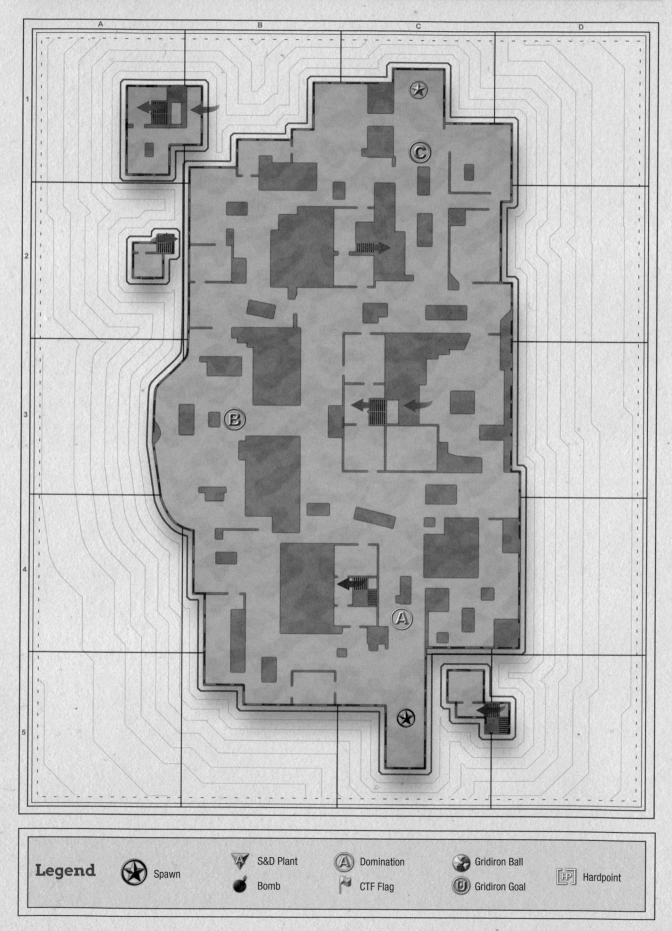

Legend

- ★ Spawn
- S&D Plant
- Bomb
- Ⓐ Domination
- CTF Flag
- Gridiron Ball
- Gridiron Goal
- Hardpoint

POINT A

The second floor of Post Office is a great spot to defend the point. Keep your eyes on the second floor of Farm House to avoid sneaky enemies.

It's hard to take this point directly from Farm Street. Farm Lot is pretty dangerous, unless you go through the first floor of Farm House. If you want a safer route, attack via Parking Lot. You can move through Radio Tower to Parking Lot with ease.

POINT B

Reaching this point isn't hard, but capturing it is quite a challenge. The only cover you can hide behind while capturing the point is the stack of boxes next to it. There's an open alley east of the point, which will make that little bit of cover useless if someone decides to look down it. Smoke grenades will help tremendously in forcing your enemies close to the point into circumstances that are more advantageous to your team.

POINT C

Approach this point from either Ammunition Depot or Winery Lot for the safest paths. The only real cover here is the truck directly in front of the point. Molotov Cocktails and Artillery Barrage Scorestreaks can help cut off enemy routes and give you a fighting chance to capture Point C. Use Molotovs to cut off one of the routes into Winery Street and use the Artillery Barrages to cut off the Ammunition Depot or Winery Lot.

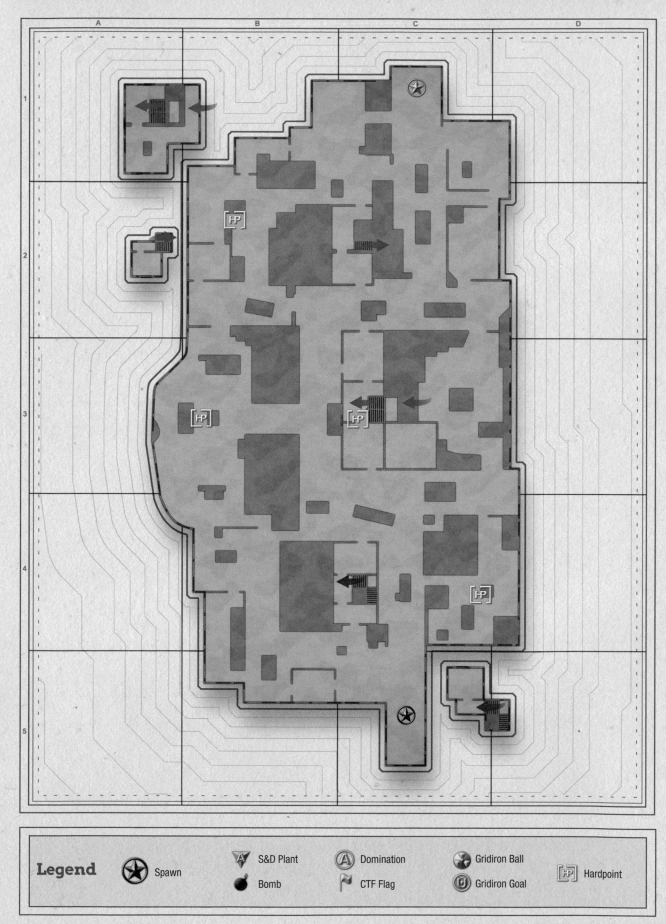

Legend

⊛ Spawn

⬥ S&D Plant

● Bomb

Ⓐ Domination

⚑ CTF Flag

◉ Gridiron Ball

◉ Gridiron Goal

[HP] Hardpoint

POST OFFICE & RESTAURANT HARDPOINT

This Hardpoint stretches between Post Office and Restaurant. It's tough to defend because of the staircase and the doors on either side of the building. There's very little cover and there are a couple of good ways for attackers to access the second floor without getting near the front and back doors. Using S-Mine 44s on the staircase will help ward off flankers. Your best bet is to make sure you have a wall obscuring whatever door is behind you so you can focus on the door ahead. You'll still be wildly exposed to the front door, but you won't have to worry about getting shot from behind or being blown up by a grenade that was thrown behind you.

If you're on the attack, toss some grenades into the front and back doors of the point to force defenders back while you remain safe. A solid team push on either door (or both simultaneously) can easily dislodge defenders.

The upper floor makes for a great flanking position. To reach it, climb up the boxes on Main Street or onto the balcony in Radio Tower.

WINERY LOT HARDPOINT

Hiding in the corner up against Winery Shed is a good spot for cover. The southeastern side of the point next to the white fence (the one with the tire next to it) is a solid defensive spot, too. Barrels in the center are also decent cover, but they won't help you ward off enemy attackers since they obscure your view entirely.

PARKING LOT HARDPOINT

Holding this point is difficult because of the slew of openings on all sides. If you're on the attack, come from Farm Street, not Convoy Street. There's barely any cover on the Farm Street side, but Convoy Street has a nice, long passage with a fair bit of waist-high cover from which to defend.

The wall with the door between the two entries from Farm Street isn't bad cover either. If you have someone on the point, you can hide in the right corner of the sandbag-blocked passage to Farm Street. It isn't actually on the point, which is why this defensive position is only effective if you have teammates defending the point.

LOOKOUT POST HARDPOINT

Hiding behind the tower on the west side of Lookout Post is the safest spot from which to hold the Hardpoint, but you will have limited visibility and the risk of getting dusted by grenade spam. The yellow barrels on the front end of the tower also provide good cover, as long as you watch the alley leading from Main Street.

CAPTURE THE FLAG TACTICS

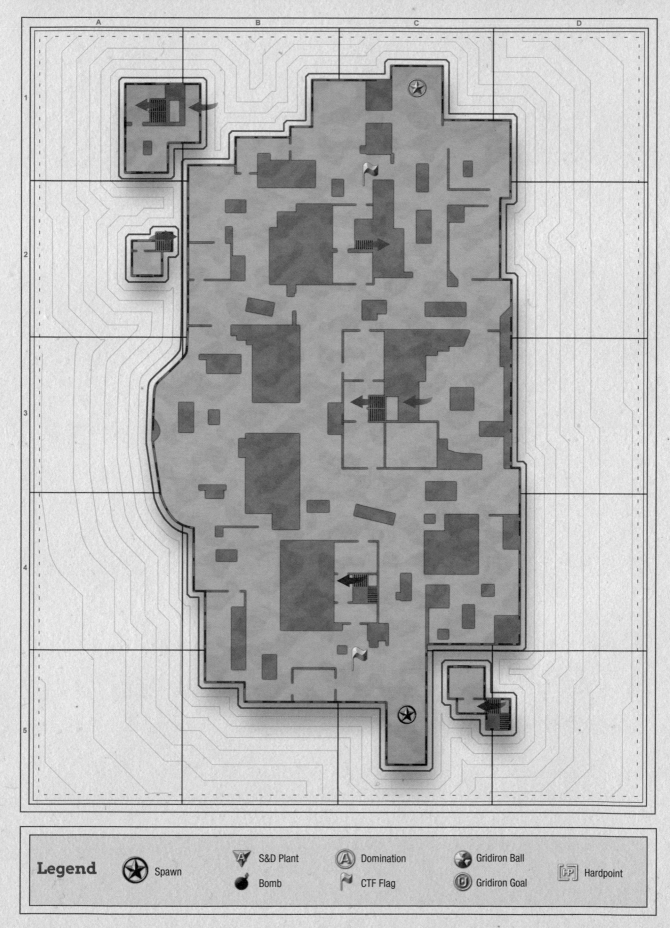

Legend — Spawn | S&D Plant | Domination | Gridiron Ball | Hardpoint
Bomb | CTF Flag | Gridiron Goal

This is a tough CTF map for actually capturing flags. The long open spaces mean you're an easy target for a decent period of time during your run back to your base.

There aren't a lot of tricky paths you can take to quickly break line of sight and the ones that are there will dump you right onto one of the main streets. Your success on this map depends on how well you use your fundamentals and how well your team coordinates its attacks. Stay off the main roads while the flag is in your possession. Run through buildings and up the side lanes of the map. When you see an obstacle ahead, run around it and put it directly behind you to limit back attack opportunities. If your teammate has the flag, stay with them and watch their back and flank while they run the flag back to your base.

These are all very standard strategies that work for pretty much any Capture the Flag map, but the most effective strategies will be ones communicated between you and your teammates. If your team has a sniper who can hold down any of the main roads, you'll be able to make your way back to the base much faster. Teammates running interference will prevent you from getting flanked while taking the safer route. A good defense back at your own flag will prevent ambushes upon your arrival at your base. Talk to your teammates and make the big plays happen to win this game mode on this map.

SEARCH & DESTROY MAP

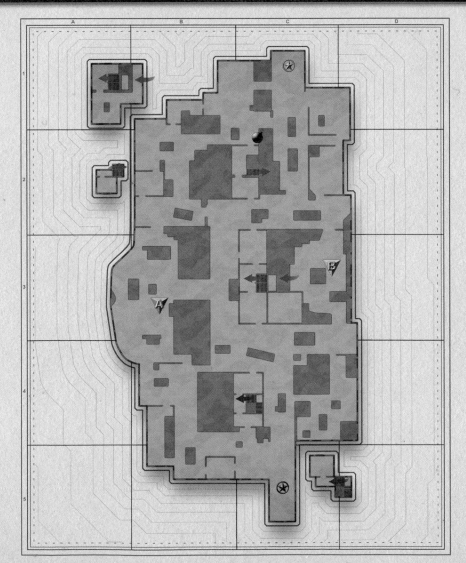

WAR

War is an objective-based game mode with multiple objectives to complete or prevent from being completed, depending on which side of the conflict you're on. If you're attacking, your job is to complete objectives until you've taken the territory and won the round. As the defender, you must prevent attackers from accomplishing their goals at every turn. During most games of War, you'll find that one side does the attacking while the other side does the defending, but this is definitely not exclusive. There are times where the roles will reverse on an objective and your job will be the opposite of what you might have expected.

Regardless of which side you're on, the timer for each objective is short and the gameplay tense. The objectives are fixed on each map, so read through this section of the book to learn about each objective beforehand; it will go a long way in keeping you from getting caught with your pants down once a proper War match begins.

One last note about War: Scorestreaks are not allowed. You must fight just like your grand pappy and his pappy before him. You'll find some Scorestreaks (such as the Flamethrower) in Care Packages that are occasionally dropped onto the map, but you should go in expecting to only find support from your firearm and your comrades on the battlefield.

OBJECTIVES

Each map has multiple objectives. Battles in this game mode are attacker-focused, meaning the attackers must push the battle to its next objective, while defenders will stop the fight if they can prevent the attackers from completing even one objective.

Progress toward objectives is rarely reversed and the objectives that can be reversed can't be undone completely. There's a massive emphasis on doing everything in your power to prevent your enemies from reaching the next objective. Even if your enemies are overwhelming a point, stay on it to contest it as long as possible—every point matters!

The objective timer that appears at the start of each new objective never changes between matches. If it says six minutes on one battle, expect it to be six minutes the next time you play that battle.

Once an objective has been captured, the battle lines will be redrawn and the defending team is forced to fall back before the out of bounds timer reaches zero.

Once all objectives on a map have been completed the match is over. If the defenders can stop the attackers at any objective, the round ends. The teams will then switch sides and the defenders will now have a chance to go on the offensive.

Building

Building is one of the larger differences between other competitive multiplayer modes and War. You can build walls, obstacles, and machine gun emplacements in specific locations to help defend objectives and slow down enemy attacks.

Nearly everything that can be built can also be destroyed. Approach a wall or obstacle until you receive an on-screen prompt to plant a bomb on it. Once the bomb is planted, back off—the ensuing explosion will hurt friend and foe alike. To speed the destruction along, throw a grenade at the bomb to blow it up when the grenade detonates.

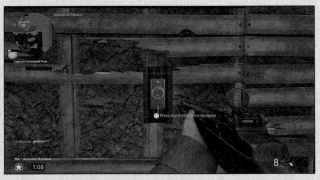

Not everything needs to be completely built in order to be useful. More specifically, you can construct a half wall to slow down enemies and allow you to see if they're trying to blow up your structure. If you build the entire wall, you'll have no way of seeing them plant the bomb, which will allow them to destroy it at their leisure.

OPERATION BREAKOUT

A
B
C
D
1
2
3
4
5
Spawn locations change based on the objective

Legend
Spawn
Breach
Capture
Build
Plant
Escort
Defend
Tank
Fuel

A small village is the stage for a brutal battle. The Allies are looking to destroy the AA guns at the back of the map, which are shooting down their planes.

CAPTURE/DEFEND THE COMMAND OUTPOST

▶▶ Objective Time: 4 Minutes

Allies must capture a building while the Axis needs to protect it. There's a buildable wall facing the Axis spawn point and a buildable machine gun emplacement that faces the Allied spawn point. Progress made toward capturing the objective isn't reversed, even when there are no Allies on the point. The Axis has a three second respawn timer, while the Allies can respawn immediately.

There's a path to the left in front of your spawn point; use it to approach the building without exposing yourself to the machine gun. Utilize the opening in the building's left wall to get inside and capture the point.

Ally Tactics

Don't wait to enter the building. If the Axis gets in and builds the machine gun emplacement facing the Allies' side of the house, it makes it significantly more difficult to capture this objective.

Use the open wall as a flanking route, as the Axis can easily come right through the back window or doorway.

Axis Tactics

Enter the building and go to the buildable machine gun emplacement on the Ally side of the house. Get that machine gun up and the Allies will have a much tougher time approaching the building. There isn't a lot of cover for Allies on their approach to the building, so use the machine gun to burn the clock down. The room to the left side of the Allied door is a really good spot for the Allies to enter the building, so defend it aggressively. If the Allies can't get a foothold in the building, they won't have a chance to start capturing.

Use the opening to the right of the front door of the house. The room just beyond the opening is one of the safest spots in the building, which will help you enter without getting gunned down immediately. You'll need to push up and prevent any Axis soldiers from entering the building in order to capture it, but this side room will help get things started.

CONSTRUCT THE BRIDGE/PREVENT BRIDGE CONSTRUCTION

The Allies must rebuild a broken bridge to press further into Axis territory, while the Axis must stop them. The battle lines divide the two sides of the bridge, so trying to get behind the opposing team is nearly impossible. Both teams must utilize the different vantage points provided by the surrounding buildings and objects in order to successfully complete their objectives.

Any progress made toward building the bridge is permanent and, once the bridge meter has been filled half way, the Allies can jump to the Axis side. Further progress made on the bridge will allow both teams to jump to either side of the gorge. The Axis has a three second respawn delay, while the Allies respawn immediately.

Ally Tactics

The barn just behind the bridge has a buildable machine gun emplacement that overlooks a majority of the Axis' side of the bridge. Be wary of attacks coming from the building on the right and the balcony on the left (behind the trees on the Axis' side of the gorge). The balcony can be particularly dangerous due to the trees obscuring your view. Without smoke grenades, this section will become very difficult.

Jump out of the barn onto the barrels below to find a good spot to shoot from with plenty of cover and a great view of the Axis' side of the bridge. Be conservative with your attacks here, however. While you do have a fair bit of cover, you are still in an elevated position. The enemy team will hone in on you the moment you fire on them.

Shortly after the bridge has started construction, both teams will be able to cross into each other's territory. Take note that there isn't a lot of real estate to work with on the Axis side, because the battle lines will prevent you from pushing into any of the nearby buildings. However, it can be a decent way to cause trouble for the Axis while allowing your teammate to continue building the bridge.

Building a little further than the halfway point, the Axis will be able to jump to the Ally side of the bridge. There's a lot more space and cover for them to work with on your side, so keep careful watch on the bridge to prevent them from crossing.

One last thing to keep in mind: An Axis player using the Airborne Division with a light weapon equipped (notably an SMG) will have the ability to drop into the gorge and use the stairs on the Allied side to get behind you and your teammates. Any other players attempting this will be killed while being out of bounds, but a melee build can just skirt the time limit and begin wreaking havoc on your team, so watch the path to the left of the bridge.

Axis Tactics

The buildings on the left and right sides of the bridge not only provide a good vantage point over the Allies' side of the bridge (and a fair bit of cover), they also house buildable machine gun emplacements. The Allies only have access to one machine gun emplacement on their side, which is stationed inside the barn directly behind the bridge. If you can prevent any Allies from utilizing this machine gun, you'll have a much easier time locking them down until the timer runs out.

Once the bridge is developed slightly beyond the halfway point, you and your Axis comrades can jump onto the bridge and fight into Allied territory. You won't have a ton of room to run about before hitting the battle lines, but you'll have more than enough to potentially lockdown the bridge and prevent the Allies from completing their objective. Remember: If the Allies can't reach the end of the broken bridge, they can't repair it.

If you are a part of the Airborne Division with a light weapon equipped (notably an SMG), run up the stairs on the right side of the gorge below the bridge, make a hard left and get behind the Allies before you're blown up by the out-of-bounds timer. It's hard to pull off, so there's a very good chance you'll catch your enemies unaware.

DESTROY/PROTECT AMMO DUMP

>> Objective Time: 4 Minutes

Allies need to plant a bomb on an ammo dump and defend it until it blows in order to complete this objective. Naturally, the Axis will need to prevent any bombs from being planted and defuse them.

The ammo dump is in the center of an enclosure that's not quite as protected as it once was, which lends itself to a lot of strategies involving repairing the broken portions of the wall to suit your strategy. The holes allow the Allies and Axis to structure their defense how they want, but you must contend with the short objective time and constant barrage of attacks from the opposing team. Needless to say, this is likely the most intense objective on the map. The Axis has a three second respawn time, while the Allies respawn immediately.

Ally Tactics

This is a very straightforward, but chaotic fight. You can attempt to seal the holes in the walls to force the Axis out, but odds are the Axis will be bearing down on you, making this difficult to accomplish. Make the attempt if you think it will help given the circumstances of the battle, but it may be better to sit at the back part of the enclosure on your side and shoot Axis soldiers as they enter.

Plant the bomb and fall back. Axis soldiers will have to leave themselves completely exposed if they want to defuse the bomb, which will be perfect for you if you're in the back of the enclosure.

Axis Tactics

Use the main street to flank the Allies attacking the ammo dump. This objective will usually end up being a complete bloodbath if everyone rushes the ammo dump, so play smart and find ways around it.

If the Allies can plant the bomb, get smoke grenades on the objective immediately—the thicker the smoke, the better. You must defuse that bomb,

but you'll almost certainly be exposed the entire time you're defusing it. Anything you can do to lower the Allies' visibility will work wonders in helping you defuse the bomb.

ESCORT/STOP THE TANK

The Allies need to walk along the side of the tank, or ride on top of it, in order to escort it to the end of a fixed path. The Axis, on the other hand, must prevent the tank from reaching its destination by dislodging Allies from the tank's sides and turret seat. The tank won't move forward if an Axis soldier is near it, which is a strategy both teams should expect to see employed frequently

If the tank is left unattended, it will roll backwards, giving the Axis some ground. Keep in mind there are checkpoints that, once crossed, can't be uncrossed. If the Allies push their tank beyond each of those lines, that's as far back as the tank will go from that point forward. The Axis has a three second respawn timer, while the Allies respawn instantly.

Ally Tactics

From a strategy perspective, there is little you can do beyond escorting the tank, since it won't move unless at least one person is near it. It's a prudent idea to push up and run interference if the tank already has a couple of Allies on it. However, your job is to hang on to that tank and never let go—at least until you pass the goal line.

While in the tank's gunner seat, watch out for attacks coming from the sides. The turret is positioned in such a way that it's extremely difficult to attack enemies who are hugging the tank's sides. If you see Axis soldiers approaching the tank and you miss your opportunity to shoot them with the turret, hop out and handle them in a direct confrontation. If you wait until they are at the tank, there's little hope of winning a fight while either in the turret or on foot.

Axis Tactics

Flanking is your best friend in this objective. The trenches directly across from the church are loaded with buildable machine gun emplacements, while the interior of the church is an out of bounds area for the Allies. You can use both of these areas for a last-ditch pincer attack.

The tank isn't much of a threat and the turret is extremely susceptible to attacks from the side, especially the tank's left. It's okay to hide in waiting while letting the tank pass slightly ahead if it means you can get a sneak attack on the Allies guarding it. A direct approach on the tank will likely get you killed. Hit the back and sides of the tank and the Allies will have a much harder time defending the tank.

OPERATION GRIFFIN

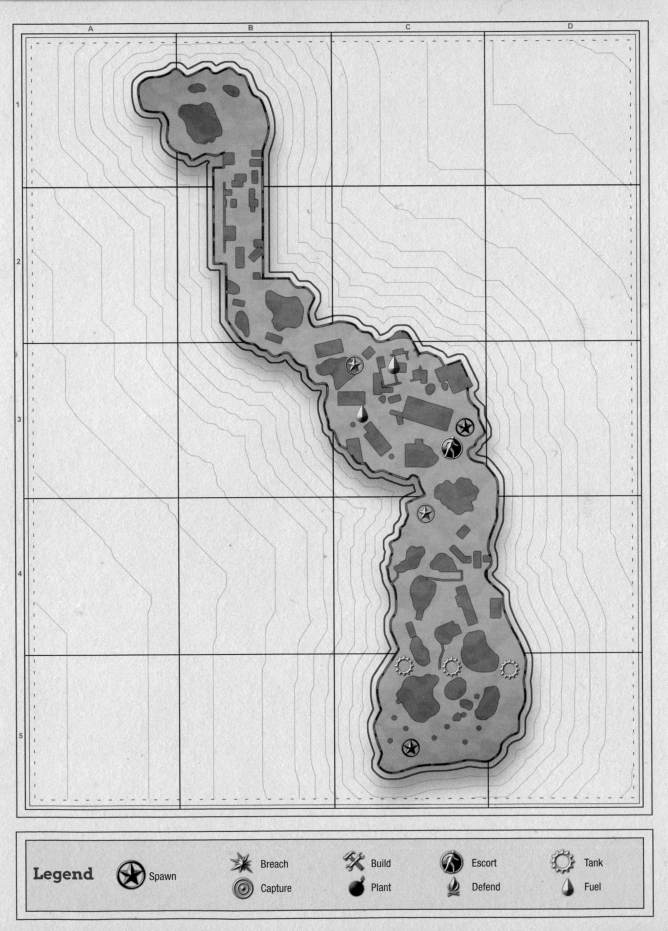

Legend		
★ Spawn	✸ Breach	🔨 Build	🪁 Escort	⚙ Tank
◎ Capture	💣 Plant	🔥 Defend	💧 Fuel	

The Axis are making a heavy push with their tanks through the dead of winter and the Allies are doing everything they can to stop them. Every objective on this map is about the Axis moving those tanks forward, which the Allies will fight tooth and nail to prevent.

STOP/ESCORT THE TANK

>> **Objective Time: 4 Minutes**

The Axis has three tanks to escort through Allied territory. An Axis soldier must accompany each tank in order to push them forward. The Allies can build obstacles in the track to stop the tanks from pushing any further until the obstacles are destroyed. Note that you can rebuild obstacles and multiple objects can be placed on each lane.

If the Axis gets two out of the three tanks to the other side of the area, they'll win the objective. Allies have a three second respawn delay, while the Axis can respawn immediately.

Ally Tactics

There are barricades to build in the path of the tanks. Once built, an enemy player must plant a bomb on the barricade to destroy it. The tanks can't destroy them, nor can they continue to the other side of the area until the barricades have been removed. It goes without saying that you should fight to get these barricades up as soon as possible. It will buy you some time and force Axis soldiers out from behind the tank, leaving them completely exposed.

You can also find buildable machine gun emplacements in front of each of the three lanes. Make sure to build them. Anything you can do to keep the tanks from moving is of utmost importance. If an Axis tank manages to get through, immediately focus on another tank lane and help your teammates prevent a second tank from getting through.

Axis Tactics

The Allies can build barricades to stop your tanks from moving forward. The barricades are built in the middle of each path, so expect to see Allies rushing out early to start building. Do everything possible to prevent them from finishing their construction. There are two per lane, so push up if needed to prevent the Allies from building them. If the Allies finish building the barricades, you must approach and plant a bomb on them to destroy them. You can't move until the barricades are gone, so waste no time in removing them.

STOP FUEL FROM BEING STOLEN/STEAL THE FUEL FROM THE ALLIES

›› **Objective Time: 4 Minutes and 30 Seconds**

To keep their tank crusade going, the Axis needs to steal fuel cans from the Allies and return them to the tank, while the Allies must guard the fuel cans. There are two fuel cans on the map, one at Alpha and one at Bravo. It takes a total of three fuel cans to complete the objective. The Allies have a three second respawn timer, while the Axis can respawn immediately.

Ally Tactics

It's possible to build two walls around the Alpha fuel can. Leave the back wall unbuilt so Allied soldiers can get through. Build the northern wall to cut off the number of routes the Axis can use to reach the fuel can. Be sure to listen for potential flanks through that unbuilt back wall, however. If an Axis soldier gets through that opening, they'll cause a lot of damage. It wouldn't be overkill to plant an S-Mine 44 in the doorway.

You can build walls around the Bravo fuel can to help keep it secure, too. There are windows and the walls don't fully close off an opening, so expect a lot of grenades and explosives to make their way into the barn. It's a good idea to block off all but the back wall and do most of your defense from outside the barn.

Use the doors on the east side of the barn to mount your defense of Bravo. These doors are beyond the battle lines for the enemy, so don't worry about them pushing up aggressively to block you out of the barn.

Avoid standing inside the barn. The openings above the buildable walls and all of the windows will make you an easy target for grenade attacks. If you want to keep the constructed walls in tact, guard the front of the barn from the outside and in the Axis' face.

Axis Tactics

This place is littered with cover and side streets, which can be a real headache if the Allies get in position and lock down the objectives. Both Alpha and Bravo have buildable walls that can really put a damper on your progress, but you can also use those same walls to your advantage.

There are two walls on Alpha, one on either side of the point. The Allies will immediately attempt to build the northern wall to stop Axis soldiers from pushing up the side path to the point. If you can dislodge the Allies, then build the wall on the opposite end of point to put the Allies at a disadvantage.

All the openings into Bravo can be sealed off, but there will still be a bit of space above them. Get plenty of grenades in there to annihilate any Allies foolish enough to stay inside the barn. Once you've destroyed a wall, watch for the opening on the barn's backside. This territory is out of bounds for Axis players, so it's perfect for Allies to mount a defensive position.

Once you've got a fuel can in-hand, head straight for the tank. You'll need to get three fuel cans into the tank to complete the objective and there isn't a lot of time to do so.

STOP THE AXIS FROM SECURING THE BRIDGE/SECURE THE BRIDGE

>> Objective Time: 4 Minutes and 30 Seconds

The Axis needs to escort their tank to the bridge. If they can accomplish this task, they'll take the objective and the battle. There are checkpoints approximately every third of the way through the path. Once the tank passes either of those points, the tank will no longer reverse beyond them. The Allies have a three second respawn timer, while the Axis can respawn immediately.

Ally Tactics

This last objective doesn't allow for deep strategy, but it demands the best skills your team has to offer. Keep the Axis off the tank at all costs and use the cover scattered throughout the area for protection. If you can dislodge the Axis, push up behind the tank and prevent any Axis players from reaching the tank again. Use the available flanking paths to get behind the tank while it's pushing up. If they get a good run going, it'll be nearly impossible to stop them.

Axis Tactics

This is a simple objective that can be devastatingly hard to complete. In order to move the tank forward, at least one Axis player must be next to it. Since the tank will mostly be moving forward, you and your team have no choice but to move up with it. As long as one player is on the tank, run interference and put down as many Allies as possible. The road to the finish line is incredibly narrow, so don't expect a lot of flanking from your team or your enemies. This last objective comes down to pure skill in most cases, so show the Allies what you're made of.

MULTIPLAYER

BUCK PRIVATE

Achievement Points	5	Trophy	Bronze

Description: Get 10 kills in Multiplayer while playing online.

This is obtained through basic gameplay. Whether you're a veteran or brand new player, you'll land this shortly after you start playing online.

RICKY RECRUIT

Achievement Points	30	Trophy	Silver

Description: Complete 21 daily challenges in Headquarters.

This one takes a bit of time, but is an all-but guaranteed get. Pick the simplest Daily Challenges and complete them.

GENERAL OF THE ARMY

Achievement Points	90	Trophy	Gold

Description: Enter Prestige 1 in Multiplayer while playing online.

There's no trick to this one. Simply play enough to hit level 55, then go to the Overlook in the HQ and Prestige. It takes a lot of dedication, but there's no luck involved.

TOUR OF DUTY

Achievement Points	15	Trophy	Bronze

Description: Win 5 War matches in Multiplayer while playing online.

Just play and win five matches of War.

DIVISIONAL COMMANDER

Achievement Points	30	Trophy	Silver

Description: Prestige a Division in Multiplayer while playing online.

Max out a Division by ranking it up, then Prestige it and this will be yours.

THE FINAL REICH

Warning: Spoilers for Zombie mode follow! Read on at your own risk!

FIREWORKS

Achievement Points	25	Trophy	Silver

Description: In "The Final Reich," retrieve the artifact.

Complete the primary missions up until the death of the Panzermorder.

DARK REUNION

Achievement Points	30	Trophy	Silver

Description: In "The Final Reich," save Klaus.

We're leaving it up to you, the player, to find out how to unlock Dark Reunion.

PRESSURE COOKER

Achievement Points	10	Trophy	Bronze

Description: During the Prologue, survive until wave 20.

This one is tricky. The farmhouse in the Prologue is the size of a postage stamp, you have limited access to new weapons, and you're limited to Freefire. On the plus side, Pests don't show up. On the minus side, Wüstlings only get harder to handle when you're waltzing with them in a broom closet. It's not impossible, but it requires practice and a bit of luck.

RED MIST

Achievement Points	10	Trophy	Bronze

Description: In "The Final Reich," get 10 kills from a single Bomber's explosion.

If you survive until one of the later waves, a Bomber might score this Achievement/Trophy for you by accident, just by virtue of how many zombies are in the area when it detonates its shell.

DARK ARTS

Achievement Points	15	Trophy	Bronze

Description: In "The Final Reich," build all variants of the Tesla Gun.

We're leaving it up to you, the player, to discover how to unlock Dark Arts.

STRIKE!

Achievement Points	10	Trophy	Bronze

Description: In "The Final Reich," knock over 10 zombies with a Wüstling charge.

Much like Red Mist, don't be surprised if you get this by accident in one of the later waves. The Wüstling often reacts to taking damage by going for its headlong charge, and there are often enough Wichts and Pests around that it does a lot of collateral damage.

LURKING AROUND

Achievement Points	10	Trophy	Bronze

Description: In "The Final Reich," find and shoot Dr. Straub.

Keep an eye on the zombie spawn points throughout the map. Dr. Straub pops up occasionally inside them, eying you ominously. One early appearance happens in the open window next to the junction box in the Laboratory.

UNDERTAKER

Achievement Points	10	Trophy	Bronze

Description: In "The Final Reich," kill the Bomber using only the shovel.

This is a tricky proposition. The easiest way to do this might be to use Camouflage and an equipped Totengriff power-up, dropping the Bomber with one hit while it doesn't know you're there at all.

LIGHTNING HANDLER

Achievement Points	10	Trophy	Bronze

Description: In "The Final Reich," build a Tesla Gun.

You must do this as part of the primary missions in "The Final Reich."

WHITE KNUCKLES

Achievement Points	15	Trophy	Bronze

Description: In "The Final Reich," survive three Pest waves without getting hit.

Practice, practice, and more practice! Every fifth wave is full of Pests and evading them without taking any damage takes skill and a bit of luck. If you plan ahead, have a teammate take one for the team and pop a 200% duration Frontline right as the wave begins, forcing most - if not all - of the Pests to pursue them and giving the rest of your squad a leg up on this Achievement/Trophy.

PLATINUM TROPHY

VE

Achievement Points	N/A	Trophy	Platinum

Description: Earn all available trophies for *Call of Duty*®: *WWII*.

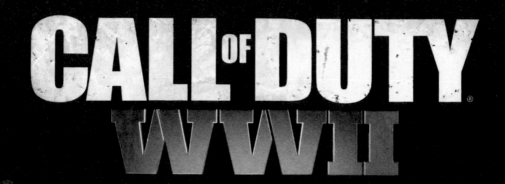

INTRODUCTION

An international crew of experts — thrown together by circumstance — are in pursuit of a fortune in stolen art. The crew has arrived at a seemingly abandoned German village well behind enemy lines. Here, they face rampaging monsters, an infinite supply of bloodthirsty zombies, and darker experiments capable of nothing but murder. There is never enough time, nowhere near enough ammunition, and virtually no chance to escape.

Welcome to Nazi Zombies. You're probably going to die.

If you're familiar with the Zombies adventures of past *Call of Duty* games, you should be on comfortable ground here. A round of Nazi Zombies starts slowly, as a few standard-issue creatures emerge from the woodwork.

The zombies appear in waves and, before long, backup arrives from more powerful and dangerous monsters. You can find better weapons and power-ups to even the odds if you can stay alive, but even at your strongest point, you're no more than a few stray hits — or one bad decision — away from death.

Don't expect to complete this on your first try. Your goal is to learn from each attempt, gaining a little information and experience with each unsuccessful run into the village until you finally have a shot at survival.

In Nazi Zombies, everything you do earns and costs Jolts, a type of energy that is derived directly from the undead. Every zombie you kill is worth a handful of Jolts, which can be used to open the weapons lockers and upgrade machines that are scattered throughout the village. However, Jolts are also required to open the locked gates that prevent further access into the village and to the Nazi bunker hidden underneath it.

As such, Nazi Zombies is a balancing act. You must kill zombies to harvest Jolts in order to stay moving and supplied. However, each wave of zombies is a little bigger and stronger than the preceding wave. It's important to maximize the Jolts received from each wave and spend them carefully, or else the zombies will rapidly outpace your ability to deal with them.

CHARACTERS

At first, it seemed as if the Nazis were simply stealing a fortune in classical art and historical artifacts. This drew the attention of the Monuments, Fine Arts, and Archives section. Their investigation soon revealed the truth of the matter: the stolen art was not only priceless, but it held the key to allow the Nazis to harness the power of death itself!

Now, thanks to intelligence from a renegade scientist within the Germans' ranks, four MFAA agents have arrived in Mittelburg to put a stop to the Nazis' necromancy.

You are randomly assigned one of these characters upon joining a match of Nazi Zombies. (You always play as Marie, though, during the game's Prologue.) Statistically, the characters are identical; the only differences come from your character customizations.

★

MARIE FISCHER

A brilliant engineer and tactician working for the American Office of Strategic Services (the agency that will, one day, become the CIA), Marie has come in search of her brother Klaus and to help salvage the treasures stolen by the Nazis.

★

JEFFERSON POTTS

An educated and professional soldier, Jefferson considers any day in which he's trashed a few Nazis to be a good day. It was one of his operations that uncovered intel on the Mittelburg experiments and he's here to finish the job.

OLIVIA DURANT

Much of the Nazis' stolen art has come from occupied France and Olivia is here to take it back. She's a weapons expert and former curator at the Louvre who regards the art as the rightful property of the French people.

DROSTAN HYND

A former art thief given a choice between helping the MFAA or going to jail, Drostan is an unwilling participant in the MFAA's reclamation efforts.

LOADOUTS

Before a round begins, you can customize your loadout. You can choose your starting weapon, type of grenades, a Special Ability, and up to three Mods. Anything you can find—no matter how slim an advantage it appears to be—could make the difference between life and death.

★
_____

SPECIAL ABILITIES & MODS

Prior to a match, you must select a role in the group. Those roles are: **Control**, **Medic**, **Offense**, or **Support**. These are simple templates that provide the player with a prearranged loadout. You should customize them as quickly as possible.

Your character's Special Ability heavily influences his/her role in the group. These abilities are the result of a salvaged bit of Nazi science, which gains a small amount of charge each time a zombie is killed or damaged. When the Ability Meter becomes full, you can unleash the Ability and deliver a devastating attack or gain a short-duration buff.

When a Special Ability is activated, the Ability Meter begins to deplete, indicating the time remaining for that Ability. By default, every Special Ability lasts about 20 seconds before it expires.

Each Special Ability has five special Mods that, when equipped, provide an additional passive bonus during the Ability's active duration. You begin the game with access to Tier 1 Mods and can unlock more by spending **Raven Tokens**. You gain one Raven Token for every Rank reached above 5 and can equip up to three Mods at any given time.

MOD UPGRADES

	LEVEL 1	LEVEL 2	LEVEL 3	LEVEL 4	LEVEL 5	LEVEL 6	LEVEL 7	LEVEL 8	LEVEL 9	LEVEL 10
Stormraven (Universal Mods)	Grenadier	Discipline	Hoarder	Specialist Training	Long Lasting	Fully Loaded				
Moonraven (Defensive Mods)	Survivalist	Resilient	Flak Jacket	Determination	Breathing Room	Stubborn	Punishment			
Bloodraven (Supportive Mods)	Team Effort	Explosive Handler	Protector	Field Medic	Dutiful Medic	Ammo Carrier	Defibrillate	Exfiltration	Preventative Medicine	Squad Tactics
Deathraven (Offensive Mods)	Marksmanship	Fiery Burst	Saboteur	Mk. II	Finishing Blow	Serrated Edge	Exploit Weakness	Vicious		

Medic: Camouflage

 With Camouflage activated, every zombie on the map immediately forgets you're there regardless of your actions. During this period of invisibility, use the time to revive fallen allies, assassinate a few key zombies (thanks to Serrated Edge, Camouflage is actually the best Special Ability if you want to play a melee character), escape a bad situation, or interact with map objects without fear of being blindsided.

Allies have no visual cue that you're camouflaged. When you're under this Ability's effects, zombies' eyes glow with a pale white light.

Camouflage is a great tool to use for your personal survival, but it can be dangerous for anyone next to you, as any zombies that were pursuing you will instantly switch to their next available target. Use Camouflage carefully or your closest teammate will suddenly get beaten into the floor.

CAMOUFLAGE MODS

FIELD MEDIC: Revive fallen allies in half the time.

SURVIVALIST: Gain a point of Geistchild when activating Camouflage. (Geistchild is discussed later in this section, under "Blitzes.")

EXFILTRATION: When reviving a teammate during Camouflage's duration, your teammate becomes Camouflaged for roughly five seconds.

SABOTEUR: Grenades are significantly stronger when using Camouflage.

SERRATED EDGE: During Camouflage, your melee attacks inflict a damage-over-time effect on zombies, dealing 3% of the zombie's maximum health to it every 1.5 seconds for 30 seconds. This takes time, but is surprisingly effective against hard targets in later waves.

Offense: Freefire

 When you activate Freefire, you enjoy infinite ammunition for the next 20 seconds — even with an empty gun — because you're firing raw, necromantic energy instead of bullets. When Freefire ends, your current weapon is reloaded.

Plan accordingly when using Freefire. Although it works with every firearm in the game, it doesn't adjust each weapon's fire rates or actions. You simply get more damage out of an automatic or semi-automatic weapon.

A useful side effect is that if you get a big enough crowd of zombies and you have a weapon with a high fire rate (such as an SMG), Freefire becomes a license to print Jolts!

MARKSMANSHIP: Your weapon's damage multiplier for headshots is tripled.

EXPLOSIVES HANDLER: You and your allies receive two grenades.

AMMO CARRIER: All nearby allies get a clip of ammunition.

MK. II: The weapon you're currently using behaves as if it's been upgraded for the duration of the effect. This is useless if you're using a weapon that has already been upgraded, a melee weapon, a Tesla Gun, or a plot item.

SQUAD TACTICS: You and any nearby allies receive a 150% bonus to your weapons' headshot multipliers for damage.

Support: Frontline

 With Frontline activated, all zombies in the surrounding area pursue the Frontline player to the exclusion of all other targets. The player using Frontline also deals double damage to all zombies until the effect expires.

Frontline isn't something you want to activate just for the sake of doing so. The damage boost is nice, particularly against later waves of zombies, but its primary use is as a tactical tool. Frontline is useful for luring enemies into ambushes or onto traps, or simply distracting the horde so the rest of your teammates can turn valves or open doors in relative peace.

After unlocking the higher-tier mods for Frontline, it also turns your character into a strong force multiplier for your team. With Vicious and Team Effort, your Special Ability results in a massive boost to the entire team's damage output. Combine that with Freefire and Shellshock for massive carnage, even against the tough late-game waves of zombies.

Frontline with Determination and Punishment may be the single most durable loadout in the game, which is handy when playing solo.

FRONTLINE MODS

RESILIENT: It takes significantly less time for your health to recharge.

VICIOUS: Your damage bonus increases to 300%.

DETERMINATION: Receive two points of Geistchild when you activate Frontline, up to the usual maximum of three.

TEAM EFFORT: The base damage bonus from Frontline also applies to your teammates.

PUNISHMENT: Zombies automatically die when they hit the user. This only gives you the base amount of points per zombie and you still incur the damage from the hits, so this isn't as tactically handy as it may sound. At best, you end up trading some health for a few less zombies in a round. Punishment may prove to be more useful later in the game.

Control: Shellshock

When Shellshock is active, your character emits a circular burst of energy. Nearby zombies get knocked down, take slight damage, and remain stunned until your Special Ability meter runs dry. Shellshock passes straight through obstacles and equally affects almost all types of zombies.

Shellshock is a great emergency option and it can save your neck, but it has a couple of drawbacks. One such drawback is that it only hits once by default. By the time you reach wave 12 or higher, zombies spawn so fast that Shellshock — unless it's used carefully — is only good for a quick breather. Fresh zombies will arrive almost immediately to back up the stunned zombies. Watch your position and time its use, or Shellshock won't work to its fullest possible extent.

Shellshock with Exploit Weakness can set up late-game waves of zombies for quick, decisive kills especially if you coordinate with buddies who have Frontline and Freefire. It's particularly useful for point defense.

SHELLSHOCK MODS

BREATHING ROOM: Shellshock gains a 200% bonus to its knockback effect and a 150% bonus to its radius. Its visual indicator is a little misleading here, as it can — and will — hit zombies that are seemingly well outside its range.

PROTECTOR: Allies hit with Shellshock gain a point of Geistchild.

FIERY BURST: Zombies hit by Shellshock are set on fire. They suffer damage equal to 3% of their maximum HP every 1.5 seconds for the next 30 seconds.

EXPLOIT WEAKNESS: Zombies stunned by Shellshock take triple damage.

DEFRIBRILLATE: Any fallen allies within range of Shellshock are instantly revived.

Universal Mods

Instead of affecting Special Abilities, these mods affect your base skills, allow you to start with or accumulate greater resources, or otherwise provide passive benefits.

GRENADIER: Carry a maximum of eight grenades, rather than four.

FULLY LOADED: You receive a 50% bonus to your weapons' maximum ammo pool.

PREVENTATIVE MEDICINE: Your entire team takes longer to bleed out. This does not stack if more than one player uses it.

DUTIFUL MEDIC: While reviving fallen teammates, you can take a single hit from a zombie for no damage.

DISCIPLINE: You receive an increase to weapon accuracy and damage while crouching and in a prone position. A Freefire user with a crew to watch his/her back could get a lot of use out of this.

FINISHING BLOW: You inflict double melee damage against zombies that have less than half health.

HOARDER: You get a fifth Blitz slot. This sounds good but, in practice, it's rarely useful.

FLAK JACKET: You take no damage from your own explosives. This sounds better than it is, as you already take very little damage from your own grenades, but this comes in handy when fighting later waves. Being able to stand on top of your own primed grenades or minefields is a valuable way to buy some breathing room.

STUBBORN: Keep all your Blitzes after being revived for the first time.

SPECIALIST TRAINING: In normal circumstances, the cost required to use a Special Ability increases each time the player uses a Special. With this mod, the increase in cost is lessened. Successive Special Abilities still increase in cost, but less so with Specialist Training.

GEISTCHILDED UP: You begin the match with three points of Geistchild. This Geistchild is "free" and having it does not affect the Panzerblitz machine's prices.

This is probably the single most useful mod during the process of learning the game, but it can be safely abandoned once you're comfortable with your skills.

RESOURCEFUL: You enjoy an increased chance to spawn power-ups when killing zombies.

PACK MULE: You can carry a third primary weapon. Note that this doesn't let you switch between weapons any faster, so you need to hammer the switch button to cycle through your arsenal.

This comes in handy later in the game, as it means you don't have to give up a weapon slot in order to carry around a certain plot-relevant item.

POWER-UPS

Some zombies and supply drops turn out to have a prize inside: power-ups! These powerful bonuses can turn the tide of a battle in a second. At the same time, though, they require some forethought to be used most effectively.

Power-ups can drop from a freshly killed zombie, at which time they appear as a giant glowing icon. Otherwise, they can be found in Supply Drops and equipped from your inventory as part of your loadout. Power-ups that spawn in the world only last 25 seconds and flash for 10 seconds before disappearing. When you pick up or use a power-up in cooperative play, its effect automatically extends to all teammates regardless of their distance from you or their current status.

UNIVERSAL POWER-UPS
Elektromagnet

Any Jolts earned from any source (including mission objectives) are doubled for 30 seconds. This becomes most crucial early in the game when you're low on resources. Don't be afraid to let this power-up linger for a few seconds until you're in a better position to use it. The break between

Elektromagnet (Double Jolts)

waves of zombies lasts just long enough for power-ups to expire, so picking it up at the end of a wave simply wastes it. Since the player's Special Meter grows based on the number of Jolts earned by the player (with the exception of points shared between players), Elektromagnet has the added benefit of essentially doubling the player's meter growth for 30 seconds.

Totengriff

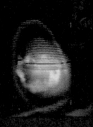

One shot, one kill! During the Totengriff effect, standard zombies all drop after one hit. That hit can come from a bullet, an explosion, the wave of force spawned by Shellshock, or your shovel.

Totengriff provides a fun way to get out of a bind or polish off the last few zombies in a wave, but it does come with a significant drawback. If you mow down a wave of zombies with firearms while Totengriff is active, every zombie is worth at most 60 points. You can get easy 130-point kills with your shovel, though. More powerful zombies, such as Wüstlings and Brenners, are utterly unaffected by Totengriff.

Totengriff (Instant Kill)

Taschen Voll

Your team's ammunition supply instantly maxes out, including grenades and your guns' magazines and chambers. In addition to dropping from zombies, you automatically receive a Taschen Voll as a reward for surviving every fifth wave of zombies.

Wait to pick up a Taschen Voll until you've emptied your gun(s), as it skips the need for you to reload. If you have to, cancel your reload animation by switching weapons.

Taschen Voll (Max Ammo)

Überladen

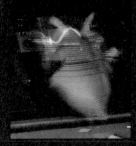

You and your teammates receive 100% Special Ability meter. If you grab an Überladen while already under the effect of your Special Ability, its duration is appropriately extended.

Ordinarily, your Special Ability meter is locked at 100% and any meter you gain over that amount is simply wasted. However, picking up Überladen power-ups lets you overfill the meter to a maximum of 200%! This also extends the duration of your Special Ability's effects up to twice as long.

Überladen (Full Meter)

If you're playing Shellshock, this isn't particularly valuable; any zombies you catch in your burst are likely to be dead well before the stun expires. With the other three Special Abilities, though, Überladen is worth keeping in mind. There's a random element to it, of course, but if you sit on a full Special Ability meter, you have the chance for an additional 20 seconds of effectiveness if you find another one.

Vernichten

When you pick up this "nuke," all nearby zombies are instantly destroyed. You gain a flat sum of 400 Jolts for killing zombies with Vernichten, regardless of how many are killed so be careful about picking one up. Also, a Vernichten only works on Wichts, Pests, and Bombers. More powerful zombies may get knocked over, but are otherwise unaffected.

Vernichten (Nuke)

INVENTORY POWER-UPS

As noted previously, these are found in Supply Drops and equipped as part of your standard load-out. Each player can only activate a Consumable once per wave and once they're consumed, they're gone for good. Their quality level determines how often they can be used before they're exhausted.

Refund Coupon

Activate this power-up and the next time you make a purchase from a weapons locker, you're automatically refunded 25% of the purchase price.

Blitz Machine Coupon

As with the Refund Coupon, this refunds 25% of the cost of a Blitz.

Flamethrower

This equips a Flamethrower, which you can use until it's expended. Once equipped, you have 30 seconds to use the Flamethrower. Zombies hit with its flame jet are set aflame and burn rapidly, suffering damage over time until they expire. This is still a rapid, hard-hitting way to deal with a crowd.

Bazooka

This equips a Bazooka, which you can use until it's expended. It only lasts for 30 seconds with infinite ammunition once it's employed, despite its on-screen ammo counter. It inflicts heavy damage to its target, has mediocre splash damage, and using it at point-blank range is suicidal.

Weapon Guarantees

Use a Weapon Guarantee to force the Mystery Box to cough up a matching weapon. You can find Weapon Guarantees for the Lewis, MG 15, MG 42, Bren, M1903, Karabin, and Toggle Action.

SCORING & JOLTS

Hold to open Laboratory
Cost: 1500 Jolts

You need Jolts to progress through the story and acquire upgrades. You can acquire a few here and there as a bonus from accomplishing various goals, but the primary source comes from beating them out of the undead. Each zombie is animated by the same peculiar energy, which you can harness and collect.

SCORING TABLE

SCORE	ACTION
0	Kill a zombie with a trap.
10	Cause non-fatal damage to a zombie via any method.
50	Kill a standard zombie.
100	Kill a zombie with a headshot.
100	Complete a story action.
130	Kill a zombie with a melee swing.
200	Kill a Wüstling.
750	Kill a Brenner.

By itself, a standard zombie coughs up 50 Jolts. You receive a bonus of 10 Jolts for any attack that successfully hits a zombie, such as a shovel hit, a gunshot, or a thrown grenade. So if you kill a zombie with one hit, it's worth 60 Jolts.

For weapons that fire multiple rounds at once (such as shotguns or burst-fire rifles), each bullet or pellet that hits a target is worth 10 points. There's no "cooldown" on Jolts; if you hit a zombie with multiple attacks at once, or hit multiple zombies with the same attacks, you receive all the earned Jolts at once.

To maximize your Jolts, be careful about the methods you choose to kill zombies. Ideally, soften up a target with a few shots to its center mass before finishing it off with a headshot or a blow from the shovel. By taking this approach, a 50 Jolt zombie can be worth 160 to 200 Jolts.

A zombie that dies due to an area-of-effect attack (such as a grenade or mine) only nets the base 50 Jolts. You may want to reach for your explosives when you see several zombies approaching in a tight group, but this tactic can hit you right in the Jolt pocketbook.

A similar warning applies to the various traps scattered throughout Mittelburg, particularly once you enter the Laboratory and Morgue. Traps are powerful tools for zombie disposal and can take down dozens of zombies, particularly if you pair the traps with distraction or control techniques like Frontline or a Jack-in-the-Box lure. However, any zombie that dies due to a trap results in 0 (zero) Jolts. It's important to note that it also costs Jolts to use traps!

Finally, all of these concerns fly straight out the window once you reach the later waves. Starting at around wave 12, zombies start coming thick and fast, so the act of simply surviving should result in enough Jolts to get any remaining upgrades. By the time you hit wave 18 or higher, don't hesitate to spend Jolts on traps, ammunition, or other incidental cash sinks. You will need every advantage possible.

In short: Be thrifty early on, so you can afford to be a spendthrift in the later waves.

BLITZES

Blitz Machines are a triumph of necro-science. If not for the subsequent death and unholy resurrection of most of the personnel involved, they would have become a cornerstone of the German war effort. You can find Blitz Machines in several locations throughout the village, ready to provide upgrades in exchange for a significant number of Jolts. A Blitz provides a powerful, permanent, and passive bonus.

By default, a single character can hold and benefit from four Blitzes (five, if you take the Hoarder Mod). Newly acquired Blitzes will overwrite the oldest ones and you can't take a single Blitz more than once. However, if you're incapacitated by damage, you run the risk of losing your Blitzes. If you bleed out, you gradually approach a point where your Blitzes vanish one by one.

While paying into a Blitz Machine, you become vulnerable for a few seconds as your character receives the upgrade. Just remember that you are locked in an animation while receiving the blitz, so it's not possible to find cover for safety.

GEISTCHILD

COST: 500

EFFECT: EACH HIT OF GEISTCHILD NEGATES ONE LETHAL INCOMING ATTACK THAT WOULD OTHERWISE HAVE KILLED YOU, AT THE COST OF THE GEISTCHILD.

Your current amount of Geistchild is represented by up to three gray shield icons on your character portrait.

It's always important to have Geistchild but, at best, it's a stay of execution. Geistchild gets destroyed quickly if you get cornered or surrounded. It's a last shot at survival, not a security blanket.

Every time you purchase Geistchild from a Geistchild machine, its cost increases by 500. Acquiring Geistchild via other means, such as the Geistchilded Up or Bolster Morale Mods, doesn't affect the cost.

FAUSTBLITZ

COST: 2000

EFFECT: DEAL MORE DAMAGE IN MELEE.

If you want to be a shovel ninja, then take this along with all the melee-influencing mods you can find. With this blitz, the shovel will one-hit kill all non-special zombies until round 16 is reached.

KUGELBLITZ

COST: 2000

EFFECT: DOUBLES THE RATE OF FIRE, WHICH ALSO DOUBLES WEAPON DAMAGE.

Kugelblitz isn't a massive improvement, but it's quite noticeable. By the time you reach the later waves of enemies, you want every advantage possible. Fortunately, it's also one of the easiest Blitzes to find.

LAUFENBLITZ

COST: 2000

EFFECT: MOVE 7% FASTER BY DEFAULT AND YOUR STAMINA NO LONGER DEPLETES WHILE SPRINTING.

Much like Kugelblitz, Laufenblitz's effects are a bit subtle, but it's worth taking for any character regardless of his or her intended role. Sooner or later, you're always going to end up running for your life!

LEBENBLITZ

COST: 500/1500

EFFECT: IF PLAYING SOLO, YOUR CHARACTER AUTO-REVIVES UP TO THREE TIMES BEFORE THE BLITZ RUNS OUT. IN A GROUP, YOU REVIVE FALLEN TEAMMATES ROUGHLY TWICE AS FAST.

This Blitz Machine is in the starting area, so it's worth acquiring early on just to be safe. You may want to ditch it unless you're a Medic, as better Blitzes become available. This blitz must be reacquired once the self-resurrection is used. It can be bought a maximum of three times.

SCHILDBLITZ

COST: 2000

EFFECT: WHEN YOU RELOAD, YOUR CHARACTER EMITS A SHORT-RANGE JOLT OF ELECTRICITY THAT STUNS AND DAMAGES ZOMBIES CAUGHT IN IT.

The radius of the shock attack depends on the percentage of ammo remaining in the clip when reloading. Reloading an empty clip emits a shock at full range. Reloading a large clip with only a single shot missing will result in a minimal sized shock. There is also a three second cooldown.

SCHNELLBLITZ

COST: 3000

EFFECT: RELOAD TIME IS CUT IN HALF.

This is an absolute lifesaver and should be near the top of the priority list for all characters once you unlock its location.

ARSENAL

If you want to survive the zombie apocalypse, you're going to need guns. You begin a round of Nazi Zombies with the weapons you're entitled to by your rank. At the start of the game, this includes a pocketful of grenades and a sidearm (typically a P-08 pistol). By taking out the first few waves of zombies, you can accumulate Jolts and use them to purchase something better from the weapon lockers scattered throughout Middelberg.

YOUR SHOVEL AND YOU: A ZOMBIE KILLER'S GUIDE

The first weapon you acquire in the Prologue stage, the trusty Shovel, is a useful, albeit limited, cornerstone of your Nazi Zombies tactics. You can switch to the Shovel at any time and wield it as a primary weapon, or swing it as your melee attack. Regardless, after the first few waves it takes a few shovel hits to kill even a weak zombie, but it does stun them for a second on impact. You can also use a quick shovel hit to knock off a zombie's helmet, setting it up for a headshot. Remember that melee kills are worth 130 Jolts, while a gun kill results in just 100 Jolts.

Vernichten (Nuke)

A heavy swing with a Shovel can kill a standard zombie (a Wicht) in one hit, as your character pries off the zombie's head. This is satisfying, a guaranteed kill, and has a chance of rewarding you with some extra Jolts (usually 50 to 200), some scavenged ammunition (approximately one spare magazine's worth for every gun you're carrying), or "lethal equipment" (a grenade).

However, as a trade-off, the decapitation animation cannot be interrupted once it starts, making you vulnerable during the process. If you want to go around digging zombies' heads off, only hit the lone survivors and occasional stragglers. If you try to methodically shovel a pack of zombies to death, you might get one before the rest kill you.

STARTING WEAPONS

At the start of your Nazi Zombies career, you have your pick of a single gun. As you gain EXP and rank up, you unlock access to better starting weapons, which gives you a big boost in killing potential straight out of the gate.

Your choice of weapon mostly comes down to personal preference. Pistols are accurate and come with a large stock of ammunition, but they don't pack a lot of punch. If you're good enough to regularly score head shots, you may favor them as a go-to weapon.

Shotguns are good for up-close combat and are lucrative, as each pull of the trigger fires several pellets, each of which counts as its own attack for scoring purposes. They have a very short effective range, however, and it's easy to pick one up from weapons lockers.

Assault rifles have range, speed, and flexibility on their side and are the best choice for a Freefire specialist but demand accuracy in order to get results, and the individual rounds tend to be on the weak side. As is the case in Multiplayer Mode, you should fire short, controlled bursts and start popping heads; otherwise, you'll run out of ammo.

GRENADES

As mentioned previously, grenades are a mixed blessing. On one hand, they offer a lot of advantages and pure crowd control. On the other, a zombie that dies in an explosion is only worth 50 Jolts. If you actually hit a zombie with a primed grenade before it goes off, it results in another 10 Jolts.

Be careful when using explosives early in the game, or else you may end up with some "cash flow" problems. At around wave 12 or so, zombies will appear in larger groups so you can go nuts.

There are five types of grenades in Nazi Zombies as part of your loadout. Once you enter a match with your grenade choice, you must stick with that choice for the duration of the match. Each grenade type is valuable in its own way, although throwing knives are a little questionable compared to the others. Ultimately, your choice comes down to your personal preference and your role in the group.

Grenades don't appear in weapon lockers. Once a match begins, the only ways to reload grenades are by drops from heavy shovel kills or the Taschen Voll power-up. You also receive one "free" grenade every time you survive a wave of zombies.

MK. 2 Fragmentation

There's a reason it's a classic. Frag grenades have a five-second fuse and bounce fairly realistically. With the proper throw, you can toss a frag grenade around a corner or over obstacles. It can also ricochet off a zombie's skull and detonate harmlessly in an empty room. If you're really unlucky, a zombie may kick it back at you.

So even if you're in a late wave and an explosion won't outright kill a zombie, there is still a good chance the resulting explosion will cripple it or at least knock it down. Lastly, you can "cook" a frag grenade by holding down the Throw button, ensuring the detonation will go off when you want.

Sticky Bombs

A sticky bomb, as one might imagine, hits its target (a wall, a zombie, a teammate) and, well, sticks there until it detonates. It inflicts about as much damage in a similar radius as a frag grenade and has a two-second fuse.

It's easy to guarantee a hit with a sticky bomb. When using one against a charging horde of zombies, try to throw the sticky bomb so it lands toward the back of an oncoming horde.

Satchel Charges

It takes a second for satchel charges to become active once they're placed. Once live, you can manually detonate them by double-tapping the Reload button. Satchel Charges do not expire once placed, which makes them excellent for setting traps or reinforcing a perimeter. For sheer tactical utility, Satchel Charges are arguably your best option.

Bouncing Betties

Mines take a second to arm once they've been set and their placement can be finicky. They don't always appear exactly where you're standing when you push the button; instead, they are placed where you're standing when the mine-laying animation completes. When a Bouncing Betty detonates, it springs into the air and sprays shrapnel over a small surrounding area. For raw damage, mines are on the low end of the explosive spectrum. They have a nasty habit of producing crawler zombies rather than dead ones, but they're crucial for point defense. If you know where the zombies are coming from, then use some Bouncing Betties and you won't regret it.

Throwing Knives

If you decide to roll out with a brace of throwing knives, you've traded the utility and crowd control of the other options for pure, single-target damage. A single knife is enough to drop a standard zombie; you receive 130 Jolts for the kill. If you miss, simply pick it up and reuse it. As in Multiplayer Mode, knives also offer a powerful, last-ditch defensive option if and when an enemy attacks while you're reloading.

Knives get significantly less useful as the game progresses, since zombies' health pools increase. You can use throwing knives to farm easy Jolts at the start of the game by dropping the more powerful zombies with just a few hits. The tougher the zombies get, however, the less useful knives become.

Jack-in-the-Box

The final type of grenade only appears as a relatively common drop from Mystery Boxes. Once acquired, Jack-in-the-Boxes have their own designated button and your supply is tracked in your UI. You begin with three and can acquire more from Taschen Voll power-ups.

When used, Jack-in-the-Boxes get thrown to the ground in a similar fashion to satchel charges. On contact, they emit a jaunty song, drawing in nearby zombies, before the box ultimately explodes. No zombie is immune to the distraction from a Jack-in-the-Box.

Jack-in-the-Boxes don't go far when thrown. If they hit something in mid-air, they instantly drop to the ground. This means they aren't great as a decoy if you're trying to get out of a corner. You're more likely to bounce one off a nearby zombie's face and get caught in your own explosion. The Box is also built so low to the ground that it tends to create a lot of crawler zombies when it explodes. If you want to ensure maximum body count, back up the Jack-in-the-Box with a couple of sticky bombs or a Satchel Charge.

It's worth spending extra Jolts on the Mystery Box early on in an attempt to farm Jack-in-the-Boxes. Much like other grenades, don't use them indiscriminately. As you progress through the game, point defense and distraction tactics become more vital. It's at this point that Jack-in-the-Boxes shine. Having the ability to distract part of a zombie horde for a few crucial seconds is absolute gold.

Mystery Math

The appearance of the Jack-in-the-Box from the Mystery Box isn't as random as you might think. Under the hood, there's a 5% initial chance (rounding up) that a Jack-in-the-Box spawns from the Box and that increases by 15% every time a player pays into the Mystery Box. Once a Jack-in-the-Box appears, the chance resets to zero.

In Co-op Mode, you can efficiently farm a Jack-in-the-Box for at least one player by having multiple players pay into the Mystery Box in a row. There is a risk of resetting the Box, but it's easy enough to find again and it's well worth the effort.

MYSTERY BOXES

The humble and powerful Mystery Box makes a triumphant return to the fray in Nazi Zombies. Look for it as soon as you get the bunker door open. In exchange for 1,000 Jolts, you can obtain a randomly selected weapon. It can include:

Any firearm you can get from the weapons lockers in the village.

Another weapon that's available in other game modes (for example, the Lewis machine gun or Toggle Action shotgun).

Other unique toys, such as the Jack-in-the-Box or the Flinegerfaust (a "rocket revolver").

If you've obtained and equipped a Weapon Guarantee power-up, use it to force the Mystery Box to cough up a specific weapon. Remember, though, that you still must pay 1,000 Jolts. In any case, the weapon in question only lasts for a few seconds before it disappears, so grab it quickly.

LMGs in Nazi Zombies

As you may have noticed, the only way to get a light machine gun (LMG) in Nazi Zombies is through a Mystery Box. It's worth picking one up, especially if you're running with Freefire!

A Mystery Box can only be used a few times before it's disabled, at which point it reappears somewhere else in the village. Spawn points for it include the following:

The front room in the Bunker.

The near side of the Bridge next to the Tower gate.

In the small courtyard in the Riverside with the Bouncing Betty trap.

As you may expect, a Mystery Box is almost always a roll of the dice. You may end up with a gun that you couldn't get in any other way, or you may get something that's currently useless. Do you feel lucky?

WEAPON LOCKERS

The Nazis have left a wide assortment of firearms scattered throughout the village. Unfortunately, they are also responsible firearm owners and have secured them all inside lockers that only open when fed a certain amount of Jolts.

A freshly purchased firearm comes with a full stock of ammo. You can carry two guns by default (three with the Mule Kick mod) and picking up a new weapon replaces your current gun. You can restock ammo for your current gun by revisiting its weapons locker, if it has one, where you can pay half its original purchase price to max out its ammunition supply.

THE UPGRADE STATION

If you get far enough into the village, you may figure out how to unlock an upgrade station in the Catacombs. In exchange for a cool 5,000 Jolts, you can infuse a current weapon with Geistkraft, empowering it well beyond the limits of simple physics!

A newly upgraded gun gains a new name, as well as across-the-board improvements to its clip size, maximum ammo, and raw damage. Rifles gain a substantial bonus to their accuracy when hip-fired, machine guns weigh less and thus inflict less of a penalty to a character's movement speed, and long guns in general are less cumbersome. A handful of weapons, such as the M1911 and M1 Garand, receive special bonuses all their own.

There is a downside, however. After upgrading a gun, it's more expensive to use. You can still reload an upgraded firearm at the upgrade station or its corresponding weapons locker (if one exists), but doing so now costs 4,000 Jolts. You can still resupply by grabbing Taschen Voll power-ups or by looting ammo with heavy shovel attacks, however.

Additionally, the upgraded weapon also disappears if you swap it out for another gun from a weapons locker. To get it back, you must go through the upgrade process all over again.

Most crucially, be careful and attentive when upgrading a weapon. Once the process finishes, you only have a few seconds to grab it from the station before the newly upgraded gun disappears forever. Ideally, you should have teammates run interference while you're waiting for the upgrade station to finish its work. If you get distracted at a crucial moment, you may end up disarmed and lighter in your wallet!

WEAPONS

WEAPON	COST	DAMAGE	RATE OF FIRE	CLIP	AMMO STOCK	HEADSHOT MULTIPLIER	UPGRADED	UPGRADED CLIP	UPGRADED STOCK	UPGRADED DAMAGE	UPGRADED RATE OF FIRE	ADDITIONAL UPGRADE PROPERTIES
BAR	1500	190	625	20	180	3x	FU-BAR	40	360	280	625	No longer penalizes movement speed
Bren	Mystery Box only	400	418	30	180	2.5x	Ronnie	100	400	425	418	Lessens movement speed penalty
Lee Enfield	1600	500	300	10	50	4x	Smiley	20	100	900	300	No longer penalizes movement speed; becomes much more accurate when fired from the hip
FG 42	1600	210	517	20	180	3x	Device 450	40	360	320	517	No longer penalizes movement speed
Fleigerfaust	Mystery Box only	2000 (1000 splash damage)	150	9	45	1x	Luftfaust-B	9	54	3000 (2000 splash damage)	150	Bypasses tough enemies' damage reduction
Grease Gun	1000	135	545	30	180	3.5x	The Greaser	60	360	265	545	—
Kar98k	Starting weapon	125	300	5	20/50	6x	War Model	10	100	800	300	No longer penalizes movement speed; becomes much more accurate when fired from the hip
Karabin	Mystery Box only	600	234	10	100	4x	White Death	20	140	850	234	More accurate when firing from the hip. Lessens movement speed penalty
Lewis	Mystery Box only	240	517	47	282	2.5x	Belgian Rattlesnake	97	485	375	517	Lessens movement speed penalty
M1 Garand	1250	300	324	8	64	5x	G.O.A.T.	16	160	500	720	2-round burst fire; no longer penalizes movement speed
M1A1 Carbine	Starting weapon	80	387	15	30/90	3x	M2 Carbine	30	360	325	750	5x headshot multiplier; full-auto fire
M1903	Mystery Box only	800	171	5	50	3.5x	Illinois	25	100	1000	171	No longer penalizes movement speed; becomes much more accurate when fired from the hip
M1911	Starting weapon	50	285	7	77	3x	Bacon and Eggs	7	49	1200	285	Akimbo weapons with explosive ammo
M1928	1000	105	909	30	210	3.5x	Chicago Typewriter	50	400	205	909	—
M1941	1500	160	800	25	175	3x	Emma-Gee	50	450	235	175	No longer penalizes movement speed
M30 Luftwaffe Drilling	500	90x8	150	2	12/24	2.5x	Trips	3	60	300x8	150	No longer penalizes movement speed
Machine Pistol	500	60	720	10	50/120	2x	Red 9	20	380	350	720	—
MG 15	Mystery Box only	180	722	50	300	2.5x	Prop Shredder	75	450	330	722	Lessens movement speed penalty
MG 42	Mystery Box only	190	652	50	250	2.5x	Bone Saw	100	400	225	1200	Lessens movement speed penalty
Model 21	Starting weapon	100x8	200	2	12/24	2x	Last Model	2	54	350x8	200	No longer penalizes movement speed
MP-40	1000	110	722	32	192	3.5x	Hardly Werking	64	384	210	722	—
P-08	Starting weapon	40	428	8	96	3x	G.I.'s Souvenir	16	320	450	720	4-round burst; headshot multiplier increases to 4x
PPSh-41	1000	100	722	35	210	3.5x	Dedushka	71	355	210	722	—
STG44	1500	140	666	30	180	3x	STG770	60	420	220	666	No longer penalizes movement speed
SVT-40	750	175	257	10	80	6x	AVT-40	10	360	600	750	Full-auto fire
Tesla Gun	Acquired via mission objective	2000	60	4	12	1x	—	—	—	—	—	—
Toggle Action	Mystery Box only	150x8	171	6	48	2x	Lucky	12	72	300x8	171	No longer penalizes movement speed
Type 100	750	90	625	30	150	3.5x	Blood Type	60	360	240	650	—
Waffe 28	1000	90	1000	32	192	3.5x	Flapjack	50	350	180	1000	—
Combat Shotgun	1000	160x8	300	8	48	2x	Diplomatic Solution	16	64	275x8	300	No longer penalizes movement speed

THE ZOMBIES

The real stars of the show are the zombies. They're dead, they're unhappy, and they won't stop until you're history.

★

WAVES

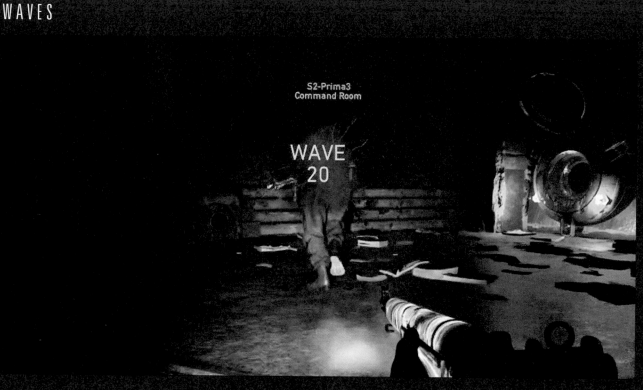

Zombies appear in conveniently numbered waves. While some of the more specialized zombies may have set points at which they appear (for example, a bunch of Bombers appear when you open the gate to the Salt Mines) regardless of what wave you're on, they become a regular fixture of each wave after the wave in which they initially appear.

In each successive wave, the zombies get incrementally tougher, more of them appear, and more zombie varieties make an appearance at once. Wave 12 is where things begin to get seriously dangerous. Plan to have accumulated at least a couple of upgrades by that point.

After completing a wave, dead characters are revived, downed characters get back on their feet, and all characters receive a grenade if space allows.

Are You Really Safe?

Don't assume that you're safe just because you're in a lull period between waves of zombies. There are several fixed ambushes that are triggered by your arrival or actions, which will occur regardless of the current wave.

In addition, the more powerful zombies may sometimes appear in conjunction with a new wave. If you don't kill them, they will stick around even after the wave ends. As you move on to later waves, it also becomes more likely that you'll run into "jump scare" zombies. These creatures will spring out of the ground or drop from the sky at any time.

TYPES

There are five types of "typical" zombies. In general, they wait to spawn as part of a standard wave until you either reach a set point of progress, or you reach a specific wave — whichever comes first.

WICHT
WAVE: 1

The most commonly encountered enemies in Nazi Zombies are the classic zombies, known as the Wichts. These standard variety are quite predictable, slow (although many can jog), and easy to kill. When fighting them alone, they're simple to defeat, although many have a bad habit of popping up out of nowhere in your blind spot. It's important to note, however, that they're lethal in packs.

As a general rule, if it looks like a zombie could hide in an object, assume they can. Zombies can spawn from any window, doorway, crawlspace, or pile of snow in the game world. If they're completely out of options, they may just spring up from the ground or fall out of the sky. Zombies are very fond of creative ambush tactics.

PEST
WAVE: 5

When you get right down to it, arms really just slow you down. Real go-getters like the Pests ditch those extraneous limbs in exchange for raw speed. In a footrace, they're about as fast as a normal player character (not upgraded) moving at a full sprint. They're also quite adept at ducking underneath your field of vision. They have very little health even in later waves, but have a much faster attack speed than other zombies and can drop a player in seconds.

Pests comprise every fifth wave of zombies. With this information in mind, set up in an appropriate area ahead of time and establish a clear field of fire. As a reward for surviving these "pest" waves, you receive a free Taschen Voll power-up, which refills your grenades and ammunition.

Pests also comprise a significant number of the zombies in every wave after the fifth one. You can often hear them well before you see them, as they're constantly surrounded by buzzing insects.

STRENGTHS: NUMBERS
WEAKNESSES: HEADSHOTS

STRENGTHS: FAST, SMALL, HARD TO HIT
WEAKNESSES: LOW HEALTH

WÜSTLING
WAVE: 8

Wüstlings, the big sluggers of the zombie world, appear as part of waves, but technically aren't connected to them. You don't need to defeat them to consider the wave "over;" in fact, don't feel obligated to do so. They're only worth 200 Jolts and it takes a lot of punishment to kill one on your own (two players or more can bring them down quickly using focused fire).

If you see a Wüstling drop to one knee (it looks like a stun animation), it signals that they're warming up to attack in a headlong charge. This attack ends in a shattering, overhead blow with their bludgeon arm and can cause an insane amount of damage. It's possible for a clean hit from the Wüstling's bludgeon to deplete a character's entire health bar.

STRENGTHS: HIGH DAMAGE, QUICK LUNGES, HIGH HEALTH
WEAKNESSES: SLOW WALKING SPEED, BACKSIDE

Try to attack them from behind. The open wound on their backside is their weak point. Shooting it is a damage multiplier that's more effective than standard headshots. It's a bad idea to attack them from the front because this enemy has damage resistance against frontal attacks, with the exception of rockets.

BOMBER
WAVE: 9

The first clue that a Bomber is on the scene happens when he blows up in your face. The Bomber is a flesh-crafted nightmare with several extraneous arms attached to a second head, all of which are devoted to keeping an aerial bomb held in position on its back. A Bomber will charge and detonate the shell when given the chance, inflicting massive damage to you and anyone within the blast radius.

A typical Bomber is slow and ungainly. If one attacks from medium range, it's trivial to take him out before he can detonate. The bomb will explode if the player deals enough damage to it or if the player shoots the bomb directly at most four times. This means even hopelessly underpowered weapons can trigger the bomb.

STRENGTHS: SURPRISINGLY SNEAKY, HIGH-DAMAGE EXPLOSIONS
WEAKNESSES: BOMB

In addition, a Bomber likes to sneak in behind the Wichts and Pests, so you may not see him until it's too late.

If you kill a Bomber without setting off his bomb, the shell remains present in the world until something sets it off. Once Bombers become a regular feature of zombie waves, you can expect to find unexploded shells strewn randomly throughout the map. It takes more than one shot to set off a shell; try to use them as improvised mines!

On rare occasions, you may also encounter a Bomber's more benevolent cousin, the Treasure Zombie. The secret to the Treasure Zombie's appearance has yet to be learned...

BRENNER
WAVE: 10

STRENGTHS: NEARLY INVINCIBLE
WEAKNESSES: GIANT FUEL TANKS ON HIS BACK, RELATIVELY SHORT RANGE

Much like the Bomber, the first clue that a Brenner has entered the fray is that your entire screen is suddenly a roaring sheet of fire.

Effectively the "minibosses" of Nazi Zombies, a Brenner is a major threat that requires coordination and sustained firepower. You can kill a Brenner with direct damage to its front, but it takes a lot of firepower to bring one down. In the meantime, he's unleashing his wrist-mounted flamethrowers all over the map. Nukes and Shellshock are effective against him, but that's the best you can hope for.

If he's distracted, you can target the weak point on the Breener: the fuel tanks on his back. Target them to cause a brief explosion of flame. Keep hitting him there and eventually the tanks will explode and set him on fire, which also disarms his flamethrowers.

Make use of distraction techniques (like Frontline) to control where a Brenner is aiming, stay one step ahead of him, and make him your top priority until he's dead. It's important to note that another weak point is their lack of effective range. A Brenner is fast enough to stay on top of you, but his flamethrowers are barely more than melee weapons. If you end up at long range from a Brenner, there isn't much he can do besides charge.

When a Brenner dies, it drops its head as an item that you can equip. Unlike most equipment in the game, Brenner Heads remain where they are dropped until they're moved.

As a weapon, the Brenner Head is virtually useless, although there's a certain fun to be had in beating a zombie to death with the skull of another zombie. However, Brenner Heads are the key to unlocking the later secrets in Nazi Zombies…

WALKTHROUGH

Play through the Prologue first to get an idea of why you're here and what's going on. The game pits you, as Marie, against an assortment of zombies and serves as a tutorial for the game mode. You can also earn an Achievement/Trophy, Pressure Cooker, for staying alive in the tutorial until wave 20. "The Final Reich" is the main game, in which the bulk of the story of Nazi Zombies is told.

As a rule of thumb, the loadout for "The Final Reich" should evolve as you gain knowledge of the map. Early on, it's useful to carry whatever you have in your arsenal (in particular, Nukes or a Flamethrower) to help in crowd control. As you rank up and unlock better starting weapons, you can specialize even further and bring Elektromagnets so the early waves of enemies get a bit more lucrative, or invest in Refund Coupons.

Essentially, success in Nazi Zombies comes down to speed and efficiency. Although you can linger in the village as long as you like (since zombies are theoretically an inexhaustible resource), basic survival can be a real concern. Wave 12 is arguably the first real challenge and the game only gets tougher from that point onward. The more you can get done in those early waves, the better off you are.

NAZI ZOMBIES ★ WALKTHROUGH

PART ONE: OPEN THE BUNKER

You begin the match locked inside a narrow alleyway with only one way out. At your disposal you have 500 Jolts and your starting arsenal. Search behind your starting position to find a duffel bag. If you happen to die and return at the start of a wave, you can use this duffel bag and pay a small fee to find the weapons you had on you at your time of death.

The zombies in the first wave are rather weak; some will die from a single hit from a shovel. Save your ammo and beat them to death to obtain bonus Jolts. Try to earn enough to open the nearby gate. Also, consider investing in an M30 or, if you're alone or your team's Medic, the Lebenblitz Machine.

The bunker you need to open is easy to spot once you arrive in the village center. It's the big blast door on the back wall. Unlike many other gates before, however, it requires power to open it.

Activate the two gas valves in the village center. One is on the right as you enter behind the Geistchild Machine; the other one is in an alley to the left (as you're facing the bunker door). Both valves are worth 100 Jolts to whoever turns them on.

≫ DANGER LURKS!

A lone zombie may appear from the nearby windows as you activate the valves.

Village Square

W

W

W

Courtyard

W

W

Starting Area

W

W

Pub

W

Riverside

Bridge

Tower

W

A   B   C   D

1

2

3

4

5

The third valve is behind a gate to the Riverside part of the village; it requires 1,000 Jolts to open. There are three Wichts waiting in an ambush pattern if you pass through the further of the two gates to Riverside. Note that they appear regardless of the wave, so be on the lookout!

The next valve is by the gate to the bridge. It's worth opening now if you have the time and extra Jolts. The Pub, which is located at the top of the nearby stairs, hosts the crucial **Kugelblitz Machine**, a necessary upgrade. Also, search for the **Combat Shotgun** in a weapons locker on the floor below.

Combat Shotgun

You can purchase this shotgun for 1000 Jolts. The Combat Shotgun is an amazing weapon to use during the early waves. When upgraded, it will become a trusty friend throughout the game!

With all three valves active, return to the village center and turn on the pilot light near the boarded-up well shaft. Doing so triggers an explosion and forces several Pests out of the open well. When the coast is clear, hop down into the sewers.

Set down a few satchel charges or mines ahead of time, then back up during the explosion from the tunnels so the Pests run straight into them.

Locate this generator.

This reactivates the gates throughout the village, although you'll need to open them with Jolts. Most notably, you can now pay 1,250 Jolts to open the door to the Bunker.

PART TWO:
EXPLORE THE SALT MINES

There's a lot to see in the Bunker's command room. There's an M1 Garand weapons locker on the wall on the way in, which is a solid, all-around weapon. The Mystery Box's initial spawn point is located near the entrance, although it's easy to miss. There's a device for constructing weaponry on the level above, near a locked drainage tunnel and the Faustblitz Machine. Also, there's a blast shield on the floor next to the door to the salt mines. Turn the crank to open the shield for an easy 100 Jolts.

To access the salt mines, use 3,000 Jolts to open the doors to the Morgue and the Laboratory. Inside each wing, you need to find a power switch to reroute current to the Salt Mines' door. Of the two, the Laboratory is much easier to find. Head through the door, stay to the right, and cut through the room with the projector.

The Laboratory power switch.

The Morgue's power switch is a little tougher to find. Walk down the hall until you find the giant electrical capacitor that forms the Morgue's devastating electrical trap. Cut through it and proceed up the stairs on the left. Turn left again at the top to locate the power switch. Pressing one of the switches starts a timer. You must press the other before that timer expires to power up the door to the salt mines.

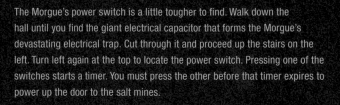

The Morgue power switch.

Reload Time!

The Laboratory also contains the valuable Schnellblitz Machine and the much less valuable Schildblitz Machine. Remember the location of the former device the next time you have 3,000 Jolts to spare, as faster reload time is pure gold in Nazi Zombies.

With both power switches active, return to the command room and pay 1,250 Jolts to open the door to the salt mines. There are always several Bombers waiting on the other side. If you open the door and back off, at least one Bomber will attempt to chase you.

PART THREE: THE TESLA GUN

The salt mines lead to an underground chamber called the Emperor's Tomb, complete with an old sword stuck into a machine. Investigate it and your character determines that the machine is empowered by the same energy that animates the zombies. You can power it up by killing a dozen or so zombies.

The task is complete once the entire room flashes a bright red color.

This is hidden a little better, as there are multiple spawn points around the perimeter and the machines' positioning forces you into close-quarters combat. The safest thing to do in this instance is to engage most of the zombies somewhere else, such as the command room, and slowly lead a handful of surviving zombies down to the Emperor's Tomb. As long as you don't get too far ahead of them, you can guide them to a location without getting ambushed by new spawns.

Once the machine has power, the Geistkraft transfer device goes live and is raised into the command room. Once this occurs, locate the big red button on the balcony overlooking the command room, behind the weapon forge. Once the transfer device hits the ceiling, press the button to send it along the overhead track into the Laboratory.

≫ DANGER AWAITS!

This next part is extremely dangerous, so it may be wise to take a break and shop for Blitzes and upgrade your weapons. You've been warned!

Now things get tricky. You need to power the transfer device by killing zombies near it. The device projects a ring on the floor to indicate the area where the zombies must die. Note, however, that it moves through a narrow, dark corridor to get there. Zombies can spawn in either direction, seemingly out of nowhere, and it's easy to end up surrounded.

You can make the trip a little shorter by killing zombies while the transfer device is moving. It eventually stops a couple of times along the route if it doesn't have enough power, but you can speed up the process by feeding it kills while it's in motion. As with the Emperor's Tomb, you can make this a little safer by killing most of the zombies in a wave in a safer area, then leading the survivors into the transfer device's area of effect to finish them off.

At the end of the track, you automatically make the acquaintance of your first Wüstling (if you haven't seen one already). You must continue to kill zombies in this area to power up another device. This eventually produces one-half of the Tesla Gun. Take it and return to the command room.

Drop off the Tesla Gun part on the weapons bench on the upper level. It takes time for the Geistkraft transfer device to reset, but once it does, it sets off on a route into the Morgue, leading up to a device in the operating theater. It's not quite as difficult as the Laboratory trip, but it's still tricky and similar tactics apply. Pick up the second half of the Tesla Gun from the crystallization device.

The Tesla Gun is great for crowd control, but causes virtually no damage and its ammunition supply is shockingly limited.

When you return to the command room, you're guaranteed to run into a Brenner, who's happily setting the entire room on fire. Dispose of him and then use the weapon forge to build the **Tesla Gun**. You don't need to take it right now, but you must assemble it to continue.

Brenner's Head

Keep an eye out for the Brenner's head and make note where it lands, as it is required for an upcoming objective. If you lose track of it, you must wait for another Brenner to spawn and kill it.

INTERLUDE: THE UPGRADE MACHINE

By this point, the enemy waves have likely gotten high enough that even standard zombies are bullet sponges. Before you continue to battle with forces beyond your comprehension, it's time to upgrade.

If you've done any exploration, you may have found your way into the Catacombs. The easiest way to reach them is through the Morgue past the spike trap, or to unlock the gate in the sewers underneath the village square. Whichever way you choose, the centerpiece of the Catacombs is the upgrade machine, which is currently blocked off by an iron cage.

Activate the disposal tubes.

There's a switch on one of the columns near the MP-40 weapons locker. Press it to activate the disposal tubes. There are a total of three; it costs 250 Jolts to enter and doing so sends you to the Catacombs, where you drop into one of three small alcoves. Here are their locations:

1. **At the base of the Tower; accessible via a gate past the Bridge just outside the Pub.**

2. **In the Command room of the Bunker.**

3. **In the Laboratory on the wall near the electrical trap.**

Each alcove contains a button; each one partially raises the cage off the upgrade machine. After pushing all three buttons, you can finally upgrade your hardware!

While you're at it, now is a good time to unlock any closed gates in the village. Doing so will come in handy later and it's worth some easy EXP. If you have any leftover Jolts, feed them to the Mystery Box for a chance at a Jack-in-the-Box decoy grenade.

PART FOUR:
THE RIGHT HAND OF GOD

Open the objective screen and interact with the Right Hand of God in the Emperor's chamber to receive your next mission. There's a fuse box on the wall near the weapon forge in the command room. Interact with it to reveal a random pattern of four colors. Additionally, this activates three more fuse boxes scattered throughout the village.

Once you activate the first fuse box in the command room, you have sixty seconds to race across the map and flip the switches on the others. This is a tough run, especially if you're doing this solo, so it's worth investing in Laufenblitz if you don't already have it. Next, follow these steps:

1. **From the command room, return to the village square.**

2. **Drop into the sewer tunnels and hit the fuse box outside the Catacombs.**

3. **Run through the Catacombs to the Riverside exit, activating the fuse box at the end of the tunnel.**

4. **Sprint across the Riverside to the Bridge and up through the Pub to the fuse box located outside the gate to the Tower.**

Once complete, you've successfully activated the lightning rods, which are located at the end of the road outside the Tower. Now you must defend the rods from zombies while the rods power up. If this becomes too difficult, try to distract the horde with a Jack-in-the-Box. Don't worry about causing damage to the rods when using your grenades.

It's probably wise to station a player or two with machine guns to watch the Bridge. Many of the zombies are focused on the rods during this section, so it's not as dangerous as it could be, but it's still a potentially lethal objective.

PART FIVE:
THE LEFT HAND OF GOD

With the lightning rods doing their job, return to the Emperor's Tomb and inspect the Right Hand of God. You may notice here that there are three protrusions on its sides that look suspiciously like battery terminals.

When you leave the bunker again, a Nazi airship arrives and starts launching rockets at your position, forcing you to stay mobile or indoors. Occasionally, blast doors open on the ship's underbelly, revealing giant glowing weak points.

Look for glowing weak spots on the blimp.

Return fire against the blimp using the best long-range weapons at your disposal (i.e., light machine guns or rifles). Cause enough damage to the weak spots and the blimp loses one of its battery packs, which crashes to the ground in the village. Ideally, try to score the final hit on the blimp when it's above the village square or the courtyard near the Catacombs, as those are easy places to defend.

When you get a battery pack on the ground, set up a perimeter around it and power it up by killing nearby zombies. It's finished charging when the majority of it blows up, leaving behind a more portable battery. Carry the remains to the Emperor's Tomb and install it in the Left Hand of God.

You must wait a couple of minutes after every successful battery run for the blimp to return. Once it does, however, knock another battery off it and repeat the process. It takes three batteries to power the Left Hand of God, which lets you move on to the next stage.

PART SIX: THE VOICE OF GOD

You've reached the final piece of the puzzle: a simple combination lock. The solution is randomly generated in every match, but how you find the solution remains constant.

After picking up a severed Brenner's head, you can "aim" it with your iron sights button to shine an ultraviolet light. Shine it on one of the four paintings scattered throughout the village to reveal a bird-shaped icon and a Roman numeral. These objects correspond to the heraldry and code plates on the Voice of God.

The paintings are located here:

1. **Pub**

2. **Courtyard (near the Bouncing Betty trap)**

3. **Catacombs**

4. **Morgue (in the room with the spike trap)**

You can actually reveal the hidden messages as soon as you have a Brenner's head in your possession, which you might have done well before now. Figure out the code and input it into the Voice.

Once that is done, use a Tesla Gun to charge up the device. A single character can do this in a few shots, although it's quicker if two or more players attempt it. When prompted, walk up and activate the hilt.

PART SEVEN: DEFEAT THE PANZERMORDER

This triggers the final battle of "The Final Reich": the arrival of the Panzermorder! Its appearance also locks down much of the village and scatters burning wreckage throughout, so you're locked into Riverside and the village square with the creature.

The Panzermorder takes up enough room that it's hard to dodge at close to medium range, but it also has a glass jaw. A player with a light machine gun can stun it at range with a single, long burst. The only reason not to keep it permanently knocked down is ammo efficiency.

A player armed with a decent LMG or upgraded rifle should attempt to keep the Panzermorder at bay while the rest of the crew deals with the local zombie population. You can't kill the Panzermorder through simple gunfire, however. Fortunately, the airship has returned.

Inflict damage on the blimp to make it drop battery packs. After empowering the battery pack by killing zombies near it, just as you did before, stick it onto the Panzermorder when it's stunned. Doing so drives it away for a few seconds and causes a **Taschen Voll** power-up to spawn, replenishing your ammo stores.

Stick three powered batteries into the Panzermorder to launch it into the sky, finishing it and the blimp in one fell swoop. You've successfully accomplished one major goal, but it's all downhill from here. There is no escape from the village and the game ends when your team is wiped out. In order to actually survive, you need to find some Easter eggs…

GAMEPLAY, TIPS & STRATEGIES

Nazi Zombies is a lot more complicated than you might expect. It's a learning process and once you know where to go and what to do, a minor mistake can still cost you the match. As you figure out the game's ins and outs, keep the following tips in mind.

ALWAYS STAY ON THE MOVE

Zombies can come from virtually anywhere — at any time. If you stand in one place for too long, you're just asking for trouble. Stay light on your feet and constantly check your six. Do not think you're safe, because you never are.

TEAM EFFORT

Nazi Zombies, as a rule, is about cooperation. You aren't doomed if you end up alone, but it's important to move as a unit. If you go down in an isolated location, you may be punished for your independence with the loss of some (or all) of your expensive and useful Blitzes. Don't be a hero. Stay together, and keep communicating.

SPACE CONTROL

There are good and bad places to fight a wave of zombies. Naturally, the "good" places tend to be the wide-open hub areas where it's difficult to get cornered. The "bad" places include tiny corridors and narrow spaces (such as the Morgue or Laboratory); unfortunately, you must accomplish story mission objectives here.

As such, try to control your battlegrounds as much as possible. If there's a big wave approaching, get your team to an open area where it's easier to fight. If you need to bring zombies to an area in order to power a device, you can kill off most of a wave in a more advantageous battlefield, then bring the survivors right where you want them. Your ability to choose where to make your stand is one of your best weapons in Nazi Zombies; keep it in mind and use it whenever possible.

ONE STEP AHEAD

You can buy some time to explore or purchase Blitzes by crippling or avoiding the last zombie in a round. While one player leads the zombie on a wild goose chase, the rest of your team can accomplish objectives or resupply.

This isn't a reliable practice, however. Nazi Zombies doesn't treat the zombies in a wave as individual entities. If you get too far away, the game will simply spawn fresh zombies in your immediate vicinity. You can "kite" a downed zombie more or less for an extended period of time, although standard zombies can break into a surprisingly quick run. If you get too far away from it, though, the game will "kill" it and spawn a new one within range of a player.

MPLETED   Next Wave in   1s

NEVER HELPLESS

You may assume that you'd be vulnerable while you're interacting with the environment, such as when turning the gas valves in the village square. Fortunately, that's not true. As long as you stay near the object and keep the interaction button held down, you can keep fighting using a melee attack; you cannot fire a weapon. If a zombie bursts through a nearby window, give it that third nostril it's begging for. You won't miss a step!

ALWAYS REMEMBER TO SHARE

You can drop Jolts at any time for the benefit of other players. While the game does track each player's Jolts, this is less of a score and more of a communal resource. If you need a loan for a new weapon or a necessary upgrade, just ask a teammate and, more importantly, don't be afraid to lend out your Jolts. An upgrade for any member of your team is an upgrade for the entire team.

SHOVEL MELEE

You can use the shovel to one-shot kill all enemies in the first round, two-shot kill all enemies in the second round, and three-shot kill all enemies in the third round and so on.

MAXIMIZE JOLTS

Every bullet landed gives 10 Jolts, while kills with a gun give 100, and the shovel 130. The best strategy to maximize Jolts is to shoot a zombie a few times with a weaker weapon, then finish them off with a melee for some additional Jolts.

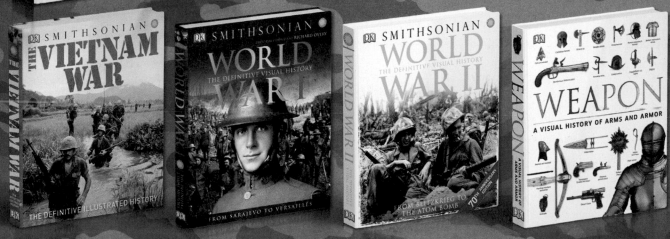

CALL OF DUTY WWII
DEPLOYMENT KIT

WWII VISUAL ENCYCLOPEDIA

WORLD WAR II

HARDCOVER COLLECTOR'S EDITION STRATEGY GUIDE

192-PAGE WRITING JOURNAL

Ronald "Red" Daniels METAL DOG TAG

CASE-REF. 07222009

WWII-STYLE FLASHLIGHT
Requires 3 AAA batteries, not included.

METAL CANTEEN AND POUCH

ENVELOPE CONTAINING 18" X 11" POSTER AND 8" X 10" PROPAGANDA PRINT

FIGHT FOR FREEDOM

AVAILABLE NOW

primagames.com/DeploymentKit

PRIMA GAMES

www.primagames.com

ACTIVISION

www.activision.com

SLEDGEHAMMER GAMES

www.sledgehammergames.com

CALL OF DUTY WWII

Written by Thom Denick, Garitt Rocha,
Thomas Hindmarch, Will Murray

Map Illustrations by Rich Hunsinger

DK/Prima Games, a division of
Penguin Random House LLC
6081 East 82nd Street, Suite #400
Indianapolis, IN 46250

ISBN: 9780744018059

ISBN: 9780744018066

ISBN: 9780744018714

ISBN: 9780744019087

Printing Code: The rightmost double-digit number
is the year of the book's printing; the rightmost
single-digit number is the number of the book's
printing. For example, 17-1 shows that the first
printing of the book occurred in 2017.

20 19 18 17   4 3 2 1

001-310212 Oct/2017

Printed in the USA.

» Credits

Book Designer
Jeff Weissenberger

Production Designer
Julie Clark

Production
Beth Guzman

» Prima Games Staff

VP & Publisher
Mike Degler

Editorial Manager
Tim Fitzpatrick

Design and Layout Manager
Tracy Wehmeyer

Licensing
Paul Giacomotto

Marketing
Jeff Barton

Digital Publishing
Julie Asbury
Shaida Boroumand

Operations Manager
Stacey Ginther